Paul Lample

In Pursuit of a
More Superb
Mission

Exploring a Framework for the
Elimination of Racial Prejudice
in America

ABS ASSOCIATION FOR
BAHÁ'Í STUDIES
NORTH AMERICA

In Pursuit of a More Superb Mission: Exploring a Framework for the Elimination of Racial Prejudice in America/ Paul Lample, author

© 2025 Paul Lample
c/o Association for Bahá'í Studies
34 Copernicus Street
Ottawa, ON
K1N 7K4 Canada
https://www.bahaistudies.ca

First edition, first printing 2025

Includes bibliographical references
Softcover: ISBN 978-0-920904-44-2
Ebook: ISBN 978-0-920904-45-9

Every effort has been made to acquire permission for copyright material used in this text, and to acknowledge all such indebtedness accurately. Any errors and omissions called to the publisher's attention will be corrected in future printings.

Cover image: Farzam Sabetian
Cover design and book design: Nilufar Gordon

IN PURSUIT OF A

MORE SUPERB

MISSION

EXPLORING A FRAMEWORK FOR THE
ELIMINATION OF RACIAL PREJUDICE
IN AMERICA

Contents

Foreword

In its landmark message to the Bahá'ís of the world dated 28 November 2023, the Universal House of Justice, reflecting on the first century of the Faith's Formative Age, reminded us of Bahá'u'lláh's admonition:

> It is incumbent upon every man of insight and understanding to strive to translate that which hath been written into reality and action. . . . Blessed and happy is he that ariseth to promote the best interests of the peoples and kindreds of the earth.

The House of Justice goes on to state that

> [t]he task of building a mature, peaceful, just, and united world is a vast undertaking in which every people and nation must be able to participate. . . . The Formative Age is that critical period in the Faith's development in which the friends increasingly come to appreciate the mission with which Bahá'u'lláh has entrusted them, deepen their understanding of the meaning and implications of His revealed Word, and systematically cultivate capacity—their own and that of others—in order to put into practice His teachings for the betterment of the world.

The House of Justice's analysis in this message illustrates this very process in memorable terms, demonstrating that Bahá'u'lláh's followers have always been a community of learners. Each stage of the Faith's development has unfolded according to the needs of the time, building upon what has come before and laying the groundwork for the next phase of its evolution. Each has challenged the Bahá'ís to attain a more profound understanding of Bahá'u'lláh's Revelation and the practical steps required for the eventual transformation of the world. And each has yielded a more united community, possessed of greater clarity of thought about the means to achieve His vision for humanity, and greater capacity to act accordingly.

In the following pages, Paul Lample proposes a means for applying that same process to the eradication of racism from the fabric of American society—a goal given to the Bahá'ís of that country as an urgent and inescapable responsibility. His intent is not to provide definitive insights or approaches; rather, it is to state that in applying an evolving framework for action to this issue, unity of thought and action will grow through experience over time, and it will be possible to advance systematically and ever more effectively until the goal is achieved.

Mr. Lample begins with a description of recent examples of such an evolving framework, including the institute process and the junior youth spiritual empowerment program, suggesting that the lessons learned from these experiences would be of benefit in our approach to the problem of racial prejudice. Aspects of these experiences include the capacity to read social reality, to analyze that reality in the light of the Bahá'í teachings, and to apply those teachings in an ongoing process of collective learning. As that learning advances through experience, the process embraces ever-widening numbers of participants in increasingly complex and effective patterns of action.

On the matter of racial prejudice, the author proposes some essential ideas. First is that modern notions of race, and the prejudices with which they are bound up, are human constructs that, while having no spiritual or scientific basis in reality, nevertheless have had a profoundly destructive impact that has yet to be successfully addressed. Second is that the problem of racial prejudice, which has festered over the course of several centuries and is still deeply embedded in American society, will be resolved neither easily nor quickly. Third, the current construct can and will eventually be replaced by another that is in keeping with the spirit of the Revelation, even if we cannot at present fully visualize it. The idea is to achieve greater clarity and impact over time, remaining mindful of the critical need for the means to be consistent with the ends—that only a unifying process will, in the end, lead to the realization of unity.

Bahá'ís, of course, are far from alone in their concern with the issue of racial prejudice. Acknowledging the deep concerns around the issue on the part of countless well-meaning and committed thinkers, Mr. Lample turns to the landscape of current discourse. While not attempting an exhaustive review, he broadly describes some of the more prominent trends of thought, together with the positive contributions they make and their potential pitfalls. An assessment of these various and often conflicting ideas helps illuminate the distinctiveness of certain insights offered in the Bahá'í teachings about both relevant principles and their application in the arena of action. The author proposes a fundamental distinction between the Bahá'í approach and those often found in present-day society. "[T]he distinctive character of the Bahá'í approach," he asserts, "is that it is not centered so much on fighting racism as it is on building a social order that manifests oneness, love and fellowship, unity in diversity, and justice—a social order in which racism finds no place."

With that in mind, and again with reference to the experience of the worldwide Bahá'í community, Mr. Lample describes a process for "creating ever-larger social spaces that manifest the oneness of humanity" and for the systematic generation of knowledge embracing all localities and individuals who are participating in this great enterprise. It is noted that in the final analysis, all such effort will largely depend upon the commitment of the individuals involved to reflect in their hearts and conduct the transformative power of Bahá'u'lláh's teachings.

However challenging the issue of racial prejudice may seem, and however dangerous, intractable and multifarious its current manifestations, the author reminds us that the American Bahá'í community is now poised to release in ever-greater measures the society-building powers of the Faith, such that "by the culmination of the current series of Plans, it will be possible to witness a profound transformation in our community and in society as a whole." Mr. Lample's contribution to our understanding will surely be appreciated by all who aspire to that vision.

KENNETH E. BOWERS

Wilmette, Illinois
5 February 2025

"All humanity," a letter written on [the Guardian's] behalf observes, "is disturbed and suffering and confused; we cannot expect to not be disturbed and not to suffer—but we don't have to be confused." The way forward has never been clearer . . . to organize these matters within the proven framework for action guiding the Bahá'í world's systematic endeavors.

— From a letter written on behalf of the
Universal House of Justice, 4 February 2018

<hr style="width:30%" />

IN *THE ADVENT OF DIVINE JUSTICE*, SHOGHI EFFENDI INDICATES that the time would come when the American believers would be called to help eradicate the evil tendency of racial prejudice from the lives and hearts of their fellow citizens. Although when he wrote to them, their community was, as he explained, too restricted in size to have "any marked effect on the great mass of their countrymen," he encouraged them to begin to make changes among themselves, addressing their needs and deficiencies, in order to better equip themselves for the part they eventually would have to play (21). For more than a century, the American Bahá'í community—first in response to the appeals of 'Abdu'l-Bahá and later to those of the Guardian—attempted to address the problem of racial prejudice within the community and, increasingly, within society. Such efforts were generally sporadic in nature, with periods of intensity and marked progress, but also with periods of diminished attention and limited results.

As new insights have emerged in recent decades from the unfoldment of the Divine Plan, the community has begun to advance in its understanding, and in its capacity for systematic action. And with the escalation of racial division within the wider society in recent years, the Bahá'ís of the United States find themselves in a position to engage in the type of action—sustained and guided by learning—that can release in greater measure the society-building power of the Faith to counteract this long-standing and seemingly intractable challenge. It is now possible to conceive how a more systematic approach to the problem of racial prejudice can, in the decades ahead, unfold in a manner that could profoundly impact American society.

The following sections explore how to learn within an evolving framework for action that can lead, ultimately, to the elimination of racial prejudice in America. The first section discusses the Bahá'í community's experience with an evolving framework for action, as it has unfolded over the past two decades under the guidance of the Universal House of Justice. The second section is an attempt at reading the reality of the discourse on race and racial prejudice in America—not to produce a comprehensive review or statement about race, but to identify a few insights that can inform the approach of the Bahá'í community to the problem. Next comes a consideration of a range of ideas drawn from the Bahá'í writings that should be part of this conceptual framework, followed by a discussion of the opportunities presented by the current series of Plans for systematic and effective action, and an exploration of the learning process that will ensure that efforts grow in clarity, complexity, effectiveness, and scope over time. Finally, there are a few thoughts about the capabilities required of those who seek to participate in such a formidable field of action. All these thoughts are offered as but one contribution to the vibrant consultation and action already underway in the American Bahá'í community.

The Nature of an Evolving Framework for Action

THE NATURE OF AN EVOLVING FRAMEWORK FOR ACTION HAS BEEN described in the messages of the Universal House of Justice over the past two decades. The framework currently employed in the execution of the Divine Plan encompasses activities related to learning about the processes of community building, social action and involvement in the discourses of society. A letter written on behalf of the House of Justice described this evolving conceptual framework as "a matrix that organizes thought and gives shape to activities and which becomes more elaborate as experience accumulates" (*Framework for Action* ¶ 54.5). The purpose of adopting such a framework is to help to formulate a shared understanding of the vision, concepts, methods, and approaches that serve as a basis for unity of thought and action in a particular arena of endeavor.

As the friends act together within a common framework for action, learning takes place when certain approaches prove to be effective, and these can be systematically implemented and further disseminated. And at the same time as proven approaches are shared, additional objectives for learning can be specified to address obstacles that arise or to explore new frontiers of endeavor that are not yet well understood. In this way, over time, the framework continues to evolve to integrate the growing complexity of thought and action that emerges as the progress of the enterprise unfolds in breadth and depth.[1] The House of Justice states that "when the elements of the Plan's framework for action are combined into a coherent whole, the impact on a population can be profound" (Riḍván 2014). As recently summarized in the message providing an overview of the first century of the Formative Age:

> By the final years of the first century of the Formative Age, a common framework for action had emerged that has become central to the work of the community and which informs thought and gives shape to ever more complex and effective activities. This framework continually evolves through the accumulation of experience and the guidance of the House of Justice. The pivotal elements of this framework are the spiritual truths and cardinal principles of the Revelation. Other elements that also contribute to thought and action involve values, attitudes, concepts, and methods. Still others include the understanding of the physical and social world through insights from various branches of knowledge. Within this continually evolving framework, Bahá'ís are learning how to systematically translate Bahá'u'lláh's teachings into action to realize His high aims for the betterment of the world. The significance of this increased capacity for learning, and its implications for the advancement of humanity at the current stage of its social development, cannot be overestimated. (28 November 2023)

Of course, what is meant by learning in this context is not a set of random actions or observations. It involves undertaking

---

1   A discussion of how to approach the idea of this framework for action that guides the work of the Bahá'í community in relation to scholarly endeavor is presented in my article, "Toward a Framework for Action," published in the *Journal of Bahá'í Studies*, vol. 28, no. 3, 2018.

well-considered action to come to understand what was previously unknown, and drawing on proven experience to determine how to achieve additional progress. It includes moving toward a selected, intentional aim, or destination, and evaluating progress to determine whether a particular line of action contributes to advancement or not. Experience generated trying to progress in a particular direction may even result in deeper understanding that leads to a decision to alter the intended aim. Thus, those engaged in the learning process continually refer to a set of questions: Where were we? Where are we now? How did we learn about moving from where we were to where we are now? Where are we going? How do we plan to get to where we are going, and what do we need to learn to get there? If certain signs of progress do not appear in a particular community, the likely reason is that the necessary capabilities and requisite understanding of proven experience to carry out that particular action do not yet exist among the participants. Learning consists both in disseminating understanding and experience of what has proven effective from one place to another, as well as in discovering new insights and approaches to achieve further progress. In this way active participants everywhere can extend what they do know how to do, while exploring how to meet new challenges by focusing on specified objectives for learning. Systematic progress is the result.

The emergence of intensive programs of growth provides an example of how learning within an evolving framework guides thought and action to produce ever more effective results, and allows the circle of participants to continually grow. Briefly, the Four Year Plan began in 1996 with the single aim of advancing the process of entry by troops—even though much of how this was to be accomplished was unknown. At that time there was no mention of clusters or programs of growth. In the Twelve Month Plan that followed in 2000, the International Teaching Centre began to learn about the creation of area growth programs in a number of localities on each continent.[2] Drawing from that experience, the House of Justice called for the establishment of clusters and for the initiation of programs of growth in the first Five Year Plan in 2001.[3] While the precise nature of a growth program could not yet

2   See Universal House of Justice, Riḍván 2000, *Turning Point* 125–39.
3   See Universal House of Justice, 9 January 2001, *Turning Point* 144–47.

be described, certain prerequisite conditions were set out, and the Teaching Centre began to explore with the Continental Counsellors and the believers in various parts of the world what the most effective approach might be. As a result of action and reflection during that Plan, the House of Justice was finally able to describe the nature of an intensive program of growth at the start of the second Five Year Plan (2006-2011), and to call upon the community to strive to establish such a program in 1,500 clusters worldwide.[4] The efforts and learning from that Plan resulted in further refinements in the conception of a growth program, including the description of a third milestone of progress, where a hundred or more individuals develop the capacity to engage one thousand or more people in a pattern of life centered on four core activities.[5] A new goal was set to strive to establish 5,000 intensive programs of growth in the third Five Year Plan (2011-2016).[6] By the fourth Five Year Plan (2016-2021), the activities in the cluster intensified even further. In a small number of the most advanced clusters, thousands of active workers could engage tens of thousands of people in efforts directed towards community building, social action, and involvement in the discourses of society.[7] There were now hundreds of villages in which almost all inhabitants were involved in some aspect of the pattern of community life. In 2021, the Bahá'í world initiated a new series of Plans, with the aim of releasing the society-building power of Bahá'u'lláh's Revelation in ever greater measure, and with the objective of establishing an intensive program of growth in every cluster in the world by the end of that series in 2046.[8]

Another vivid example of how the framework for action serves to facilitate a process of learning and development is the Junior <u>Youth Spiritual</u> Empowerment Program. In the Five Year Plan

4   See Universal House of Justice, 27 December 2005, *Turning Point* 195–208.

5   See the full description of a third milestone cluster, Universal House of Justice, 28 December 2015, *Framework for Action* 218–24.

6   See Universal House of Justice, 28 December 2010, *Framework for Action* 95–119.

7   See Universal House of Justice, 29 December 2015, *Framework for Action* 209–33.

8   See Universal House of Justice, 30 December 2021, *Messages of the Universal House of Justice: 2001-2022* 842–64.

beginning in 2001, the Office of Social and Economic Development supported a few pilot projects in different countries to explore opportunities for enhancing literacy in the Bahá'í world. The project that proved to be most promising involved junior youth, leading to an exploration of how to assist young people of that early age to enhance their power of expression. The concept of junior youth and the desire for a program for that age group had emerged—yet everything about such a program still needed to be learned, step by step. This included learning how to engage youth as animators and develop their capacities; how to attract and maintain the involvement of junior youth; how to develop an approach to service activities; how to develop materials for study beginning with one book and expanding to a dozen and more; how to work with the parents of junior youth; how to multiply groups in a cluster with the assistance of a cluster coordinator; how to organize camps or intensive programs to bring together large numbers to deepen the vision and commitment of junior youth; how to maintain ten groups in a cluster, then thirty and beyond; how to offer the program through the training institute as a fourth core activity; how to introduce the program into academic schools; how to sustain the involvement of junior youth for the three years of the program and then facilitate their participation in the courses of the institute; how to support the wide expansion of the program through a network of offices and learning sites; and, still unfinished, how to build the capacity of training institutes to extend the program, in all its dimensions, to every cluster. An effective approach for each of these matters had to be learned through action and reflection over time. In two decades, the initiative evolved from a mere idea to a vibrant program that now embraces hundreds of thousands of junior youth worldwide. And learning continues in the current series of Plans to further increase the spread and impact of the program and its contribution to the progress of society building in country after country.

It is evident that in 1996, the path leading to the development of a program of growth and the features it would attain by 2021 could in no way have been visualized in their entirety. The same was true of the junior youth program at the turn of the century. Indeed, it is often difficult at the beginning of a single Plan to anticipate what the situation will be by its end. By approaching the work of growth and community building through the perspective of an evolving framework for action, Bahá'ís everywhere were able to unite in an enterprise that began with a few general ideas and became—over time and through experience—more focused on what could be achieved, more systematic in approach, and ever-more accomplished in proven results. Rather than expecting to find a simple formula that could be replicated from place to place, a capacity for learning was raised among participants in each cluster and in neighborhoods or villages to contribute to and draw from the worldwide learning process. The same pattern of systematic endeavor made possible through learning and the adoption of an evolving framework for action—in which action begins simply, a systematic effort grows in complexity over time, and experience that has proven to be effective is disseminated and multiplied—is also readily evident in the development of many other aspects of the work of the Bahá'í community in recent decades. This includes the development of training institutes, the multiplication of efforts for social and economic development, enhancement of the intellectual life of the community, and the extension of endeavors for involvement in the discourses of society.

The experience over the past twenty-five years of learning within an evolving conceptual framework that has produced evident results—ever-increasing understanding, more precise concepts and language, and systematic action that grows in complexity and impact over time—can be best appreciated when contrasted with the sincere and dedicated efforts of the previous four decades, which could not produce a breakthrough in the challenge of sustaining large scale consolidation and community building.

It is useful, then, in order to move beyond noteworthy but largely disconnected ideas and activities, to deepen our understanding of how the evolving framework for action that has propelled the progress of the Bahá'í world for two decades can give rise to a more sustained and systematic approach for the ultimate elimination of racial prejudice. Of course, elements of the framework pertaining to expansion and consolidation, social action, and involvement in the discourses of society have direct implications for this work, and, indeed, activities in all these areas are already addressing the challenge of racial prejudice, whether directly or indirectly. But it is vital to reflect upon and consciously incorporate additional elements from the Bahá'í writings and the letters of the House of Justice written in recent years that are particular to race unity.[9]

Progressively clarifying aspects of the framework for action as they apply to matters pertaining to race, and fostering the evolution of the framework as practical experience accumulates, will help transform well intentioned and often sacrificial efforts for the elimination of racial prejudice from uncoordinated activities, shaped to varying degrees by assumptions current in the wider society, into systematic, widespread, and effective patterns of action. Although such patterns of action begin simply and take time to grow in complexity, and although many of them may appear to be only indirectly associated with racial issues, this process will not place Bahá'ís at the sidelines of the work of addressing the problem of race in the wider society. Rather, it is the essential work that will ultimately help to lead the American nation out of its intractable impasse and endless conflict. If this work is pursued unrelentingly in the decades ahead, the Guardian's high expectations for the Bahá'í community's unique contribution to the elimination of racial prejudice in American society can ultimately be fulfilled in a manner that today can be only dimly imagined.

Some Insights from the Contemporary Discourse on Race

ESSENTIAL FOR ANY ATTEMPT TO TRANSFORM SOCIAL REALITY IS A sound reading of its current condition. One aspect of the evolving framework for action, then, is to seek an understanding of how racial prejudice currently operates in order to begin to shape an approach to resolving the challenge. Too often, matters of fact are obscured by those with contending political or ideological positions. Because Bahá'ís are immersed in their society and have absorbed so many ideas, values, and practices from it, a grasp of some of the forces at work is essential to be able to begin to distinguish society's imaginings from its productive approaches, by

9   See for example a letter written on behalf of Universal House of Justice, in *Framework for Action* 279–82.

assessing them in light of the penetrating insights offered by the Bahá'í teachings. Any reading of reality ought to become keener and more profound over time.

Owing to the dominant and pervasive nature of the issue of race in the history of the United States, much has been written on the subject, and it is impossible to capture and distill here all the relevant ideas and experiences that have a bearing on the potential efforts that can be made by Bahá'ís. Race and racial concerns are a vibrant area of study among academics across many disciplines, with general consensus in some areas and lively debate in others, including on the specific question of racial prejudice directed against Black Americans. Nevertheless, even if one ignores the voices of those who, for their self-interested purposes, seek to perpetuate a hierarchical racialized system in America, there is no apparent diagnosis and remedy commonly accepted by the fair-minded—those who, whatever their ideological commitments, share a concern for justice and collective well-being in society. Therefore, the aim here is not to provide a comprehensive picture of the issue of race in America, to summarize the scholarly debate, or to propose a specific remedy, all of which are beyond my capacity. Rather, the focus here will be on identifying a few select points that can help to shed light on some of the challenges confronting current approaches for the elimination of racial prejudice in the wider society. It is hoped that consciousness of these challenges can assist the Bahá'í community to avoid, in its own community building process, certain pitfalls currently obstructing progress in the wider society.

At this time, individual Bahá'ís naturally have a range of diverse personal views on these topics. They must, of course, scrupulously avoid being drawn into contentious political debates and machinations, or bringing those debates into the life of the community. And Bahá'ís conversant with the wider discourse on race will no doubt increasingly share invaluable insights within and outside the Bahá'í community as understanding grows. Yet it should be appreciated that only with experience that is demonstrated to be effective over time will unity of thought and action significantly increase in the years ahead. As more individuals with diverse views and experiences contribute what they have learned to the conscious collective effort to develop the evolving framework for the elimination of racial prejudice, an ever-more accurate reading of reality about race in American society will emerge.

Some insight into the difficulty of agreeing on the nature of the challenge before us can be obtained by looking at varying and contradictory uses of the term "racist." In the past, there was general agreement that a racist was an individual who held a white supremacist viewpoint, maintaining other races to be inferior and insisting upon prejudicial practices that flowed from this belief. When such overt racism was largely discredited and increasingly seen as illegitimate within mainstream public discourse after the success of the civil rights movement, the focus of those concerned with eradicating racial prejudice turned to systemic racism, the way that racial injustice is embedded and hidden in social systems and practices.[10] This gave rise to the concept of "racism without racists,"[11] which emerged to explain color-blind racism and the perpetuation of racist policies in institutional structures when no individuals would outwardly profess personal prejudices. Another approach explained that racism was manifested in the form of microaggressions.[12] While each of these insights offers constructive ways to examine the contemporary impact of racism, they also exist side by side with a host of other categorical perspectives: That all white people are racist and will always be. That racism is inherently associated with power and therefore Black people cannot be racist. That one is either an antiracist, fighting social policies perceived as racist, including by imposing discriminatory practices if necessary to achieve equality, or one is a racist, whether white or Black, for allowing the perpetuation of

---

10   See for example, *Metaracism: How Systemic Racism Devastates Black Lives—And How We Break Free*, by Tricia Rose and *The New Jim Crow: Mass Incarceration in the Age of Colorblindness*, by Michelle Alexander.

11   See for example, *Racism without Racists: Color-Blind Racism and the Persistence of Racial Inequality in America*, by Eduardo Bonilla Silva.

12   See for example, *Racial Microaggressions: Using Critical Race Theory to Respond to Everyday Racism*, by Daniel G Solórzano and Lindsay Pérez Huber. The attitude toward microaggressions can vary. Ibram X. Kendi considers them a form of racial abuse (*How to Be and Antiracist* 47). Coleman Hughes, however, considers microaggressions to be overemphasized, as he argues in his book, *The End of Race Politics*, where he observes that a 2015 document prepared by the University of California identified the phrase "There is only one race, the human race" as a microaggression (61).

these social policies, even through inaction.[13] That those who call for such reverse discrimination are neoracists.[14] Some even assert that those who raise concerns about racism are the true racists.[15] Such views on racism may be echoed by those voices, alluded to above, that self-interestedly seek to maintain a racially hierarchical society. But even among those who genuinely wish to address the blight of racism, the term has been used in myriad different ways; though many such usages raise important points, it is hard to reconcile them. Are the racists those who insist upon racial categories or those who insist we let them go? How can racial supremacy be identified and overcome if it is indistinguishable from unconscious perpetuation of prejudicial practices? With such diverse assumptions and prescriptions surrounding such a fundamental term—one among many concepts that depict the current reality—how is it possible to find constructive engagement and a collective way forward?

The challenge increases significantly when we recognize that the problem of racial prejudice cannot be reduced to the relationship between Black and white alone. Of course, many statements of 'Abdu'l-Bahá and Shoghi Effendi have such a focus, which is to be expected given the nature of the problem they were commenting upon at the time. But, as the House of Justice explained in 2011, "the situation is infinitely more complex. The American nation is much more diverse than in 1938, and the friends cannot be concerned only with relations between black and white, essential as they are. The expressions of racial prejudice have transmuted into forms that are multifaceted, less blatant and more intricate, and thus more intractable" (*Framework* 281). Anti-Black racism, although perhaps the most egregious expression of racial prejudice, is not the only form found in the United States, which witnesses prejudice toward and across the many racial and ethnic groups in the country, and even manifestations of prejudice of color or class within groups.

---

13   See for example, *How to be an Antiracist, by* Ibram X. Kendi.

14   See for example, *The End of Race Politics: Arguments for a Color-blind America*, by Coleman Hughes.

15   An example of this logic can be found in Jay Bookman, "Let's Be Honest about who Really Fans the Flame of Racism," *Georgia Recorder*, 30 May 2020.

The challenge of agreeing on how to address racial prejudice even extends to differences in understanding of the concept of race itself. Is race real? In the view of most religions, and in particular the Bahá'í Faith, humanity is one, and race has no spiritual basis. Scientists have demonstrated the fallacious nature of the belief in a biological basis for race as a physical reality. But it persists nevertheless, and scientific findings are otherwise used to support ideological choices.[16] Yet, whether one insists that race has an objective reality, or whether one concludes that it is imaginary, the conception of race has given rise to a social construct and practice surrounding "race." And as a social construct, the current understanding of race can be changed, or even eliminated. Where did this social conception come from, what form does it take now, and what are the possibilities for the future?

The concepts, values, beliefs, and practices now associated with race at one time did not exist; at a point in history they were created, enforced, and promulgated by human beings. As an aspect of social reality, racialized and racist concepts have been generated and utilized in a highly oppressive manner in particular forms for at least four centuries; as a result, individuals and peoples are socially assigned to specified racial categories. The social construct of race is especially pernicious and deep-rooted. It originated out of a conscious intention to establish the superiority of one group of people over another, in belief and practice. Inseparably intertwined with Enlightenment thought, it was carried throughout the globe by European imperialism,[17] and took root in the American

16   Science has consistently been distorted to try to provide a justification for the dehumanization caused by imagining a racialized hierarchy. When the human genome project was completed, it was considered to be a definitive demonstration that race was not a biological reality for human beings. The differences in the genome of those within a so-called race were much greater than the differences between so-called races. Yet, the belief in race persists. And the new science has been employed to perpetuate the perception of "race," even by those who hope to eliminate racism. See *Fatal Invention: How Science, Politics, and Big Business Recreate Race in the Twenty-first Century,* by Dorothy Roberts. "Race," Roberts concludes, "is not a biological category that is politically charged. It is a political category that has been disguised as a biological one" (Roberts 4).

17   See for example, *Race, Empire, and the Idea of Human Development,* by Thomas McCarthy, and *The Racial Contract,* by Charles W. Mills.

colonies of the European powers, sowing seeds that continue to bear bitter fruit in the United States today.[18] Whereas it is commonly assumed that the existence of race led to racism, which in turn facilitated slavery, another perspective proposes that in fact, the opposite took place, beginning in America with the first arrival of enslaved Africans in Virginia in the early 1600s. There was a need for cheap labor in the American colonies, and people from both the European and African continents (who would now be considered white and Black people), as well as the Indigenous population, were initially conscripted to this end. Chattel slavery emerged gradually as laws and practices evolved. A need to justify the practice of slavery required the formulation of racist attitudes and structures, and so a language emerged that gave rise to the American conception of race. In essence, this was a process of othering intended to legitimize an unjust practice by dehumanizing a segment of humanity, whose members could then be subjected to that practice. Various peoples who came to the United States were also categorized by racial designations, or otherwise assimilated into the original categories of white and Black. The result was a hierarchical system of othering, with its associated forms of dehumanization and oppression, that has been maintained, in ever-mutating forms, over several centuries.

In this hierarchy, only white people could be seen as fully human, or raceless, or even as true Americans, while the humanity of others was diminished in one way or another. And while efforts to reconstruct the social reality of race in the past century have resulted in some evident progress toward treating diverse ethnicities more equally, true oneness remains elusive. The residual manifestations of injustice in society, whether direct or indirect, affect people differently. Some live oblivious of the impact of racial prejudice, while for others it may be a daily enervating or oppressive burden; and for all too many, the experience of racial prejudice comes in the form of violence.

Though this concept of race is entrenched in American society, because it is a social construct, a different construct—with different concepts, values, beliefs and practices—can ultimately take

---

18   See, for example, *The Invention of the White Race*, by Theodore W. Allen, and *Teaching White Supremacy: America's Democratic Ordeal and the Forging of Our National Identity*, by Donald Yacovone.

its place. Some, of course, for their own self-centered aims, will strive to maintain the racial hierarchy by altering and disguising its form. But there are other possibilities. One is a multicultural society where a conception of racial categories is maintained, but prejudice is somehow purged, and outcomes are thereby equalized. Yet another possibility would see the elimination of the concept of race in American society, with the unity in diversity of cultures and ethnicities acknowledged and valued.

Yet, experience has demonstrated that attempts to find a path out of the current false and virulent social division of the human family into a racialized hierarchy run into a set of conflicting considerations on the question of whether or not to use racial categories in analyses of, and strategies to overcome, racism. Broadly speaking, there is a tension between race neutrality and race consciousness, or between colorblindness and racial essentialism (framed in more social than biological terms).[19] That is, the idea that people should be treated without regard to race in both public policy and private life is contrasted with the idea that in order to eliminate the effects of racism, it is necessary to take into account the social idea of race, existing in social forms whose boundaries can be defined and whose multiple categories are continually curated.[20] While both ideas are taken up, debated, nuanced, and

---

19   See "A Better Antiracism", by Coleman Hughes. Compare *The End of Race Politics: Arguments for a Colorblind America*, by Coleman Hughes, and *How to Be an Antiracist*, by Ibram X. Kendi. It should be observed that the tension between colorblindness and race consciousness is often presented as a tension between those claiming to be colorblind in order to be exempt from taking action, and those who are trying to do something about existing racial hierarchies. This, of course, produces an untenable situation, but it is not the central issue being raised here. Racial oppression can just as easily be promoted in a form of race consciousness, by insisting upon white superiority and the inferiority of other races. Instead, as mentioned, what is discussed here is the dilemma confronting fair-minded advocates who wish to eliminate racial prejudice, but who cannot agree on a constructive path forward to effect lasting social transformation.

20   See for example, Wairimu Maureen Waithaka, "Learning to Be Black: Navigating a New Identity in Nova Scotia." See also *Deconstructing Race: Multicultural Education Beyond the Color-Bind* by Jabari Mahiri. The following articles explore different dimensions of this issue: Coleman Hughes, "A Better Anti-Racism" and Reihan Salam, "America Needs Anti-Racialism." In

deployed in academic discussions of race, the concern here is how they inform the popular discourse on race and racial prejudice in America.[21]

Before considering these two positions in more detail, a note should be made about the nature of the discourse within which these ideas are explored in wider society. As is common in contemporary social discourse broadly speaking, advocates of each of these dichotomized positions may accuse those on the opposite side of the debate of being malicious or unthinking contributors to

---

her book *Caste: The Origins of Our Discontents*, Isabel Wilkerson offers a vivid illustration of how the American conception of race is not a universal phenomenon—however much racialized perceptions are projected by western societies. She writes: "A few years ago, a Nigerian-born playwright came to a talk that I gave at the British Library in London. She was intrigued by the lecture, the idea that 6 million African-Americans had had to seek political asylum within the borders of their own country during the Great Migration, a history that she had not known of. She talked with me afterward and said something that I have never forgotten, that startled me in its simplicity. 'You know that there are no black people in Africa,' she said. Most Americans, weaned on the myth of drawable lines between human beings, have to sit with that statement. It sounds nonsensical to our ears. Of course there are black people in Africa. There is a whole continent of black people in Africa. How could anyone not see that? 'Africans are not black,' she said. 'They are Igbo and Yoruba, Ewe, Akan, Ndebele. They are not black. They are just themselves. They are humans on the land. That is how they see themselves, and that is who they are.' What we take as gospel in American culture is alien to them, she said. 'They don't become black until they go to America or come to the U.K.,' she said. 'It is then that they become black.' It was in the making of the New World that Europeans became white, Africans black, and everyone else yellow, red, or brown. It was in the making of the New World that humans were set apart on the basis of what they looked like, identified solely in contrast to one another, and ranked to form a caste system based on a new concept called race. It was in the process of ranking that we were all cast into assigned roles to meet the needs of the larger production. None of us are ourselves" (52).

21   As one writer characterized the manifestation of this problem in the attempt to overcome racial prejudice: "For at least 50 years, Californians have been fighting about whether their state government should be race neutral, treating all individuals equally under the law regardless of the color of their skin, or race conscious, granting preferential treatment to certain groups while discriminating against others to remedy past discrimination or increase diversity" (Friedersdorf n.p.).

the perpetuation of racism. And indeed, for each of these two perspectives there is both a well-intentioned form of the argument—offered as a sincere approach to overcoming prejudice—as well as a negative form whose implicit intent is to perpetuate racial prejudice in a different guise. Indeed, some have promulgated and exacerbated one side or the other in the debate to achieve political or social objectives.[22] And so, for example, even white supremacists pursue their aims through either a disingenuous claim of colorblindness or an insistence upon racial essentialism that validates their superiority. However, it is also the case that sincere individuals truly believe that the way beyond a social order mired in racism can only be found in one or the other approach: an embrace of race neutrality or an embrace of race consciousness. Even Black intellectuals have clashed over these two approaches.[23] Because of this intractable dilemma surrounding race—whether it emerges inadvertently or whether it is intentionally cultivated to prevent meaningful change—contemporary discussion too often falls into a pattern of dichotomy and debate where no one can convince another, and where ineffective or at times conflicting remedies are prescribed.

The argument for race neutrality or colorblindness, which takes different forms, proposes that since all people should be treated equally, issues of race should not be considered in social policy or community life. From this perspective, it is argued that the best way to eliminate the vestiges of racism is to stop centering the concept of race in personal interactions, and to exclude racial considerations from public policy.[24]

Those who reject such a race neutral approach feel that any

---

22   For example, and unfortunately, one of the most prominent forms of this discussion is embedded in an ongoing political debate, in which a disingenuous appeal to colorblindness (designed to maintain and obscure, rather than eradicate, racial discrimination) situates itself in opposition to efforts to broaden antiracist efforts for social justice.

23   See for example, *Woke Racism: How a New Religion Has Betrayed Black America*, by John McWhorter.

24   For example, see public statements made by the actor Morgan Freeman. In response to a question by reporter Mike Wallace on *60 Minutes* about how to get rid of racism, Freeman opined: "Stop talking about it." "I'm going to stop calling you a White man, and I'm going to ask you to stop calling me a Black man" (Freeman).

contemporary attempt to aspire to colorblindness is merely a way of denying or avoiding the persistent problems of racism. A call for colorblindness, it is argued, allows for the perpetuation of racist policies that often act invisibly or indirectly through institutional structures that maintain or exacerbate racial disparity and oppression. A colorblind approach can also obscure appreciation for the beauty and richness of human diversity.

The alternative perspective, racial consciousness or essentialism, proposes that race should be embraced as a positive form of identity. It can then be determined whether different races are treated equally. From this perspective, there is a difference between social assignments into racial categories, which might be oppressive, and personal identification with one, or even more, racial categories, which is viewed as positive.[25] The value of diverse efforts undertaken to reclaim and celebrate racial identities is self-evident when attempting to counteract centuries of systematic negation and misrepresentation. Thus, race should be affirmed and appreciated, through some form of cultural pluralism or multiculturalism, which will ensure that all people are able to foster and express their unique character. From this perspective, the obstacles to the realization of a thriving multicultural society are a legacy of personal prejudices and institutional forms of racism that continue to oppress people of color. Racism therefore must be consistently exposed and rooted out, requiring, particularly, a change in consciousness and action by white people.

Those who question forms of race consciousness believe that race-conscious approaches ignore people's full humanity, and instead reinforce types of racial categorization to which people are continually being expected to conform. Antiracist strategies aimed at achieving equal outcomes, it is suggested, are misplaced, ignore complex factors, or, in any case, add to rather than root out racist sentiments and practices.

The dilemma presented by racial categories—neutrality versus consciousness, colorblindness versus essentialism—has been explored by numerous observers. Some have pointed out, for

---

25   See, for example, *Multiracial Identity and Racial Politics in the United States*, by Natalie Masuoka, and *Racial Identity Theory: Applications to Individual, Group, and Organizational Interventions*, edited by Chalmer E. Thompson.

instance, that whether society attempts to ignore racial categories, or whether it maintains racial categories through social assignment or self-identification, the preexisting racialized hierarchy is unintentionally reinforced; in this way, even the United States Census can serve as an instrument that perpetuates prejudice and racism in society.[26] Thus, attempts to discard the oppression of racism, to reclaim the dignity and equality of devalued peoples through liberating philosophies or appeals to justice run the risk of crystalizing the distinction of race into fixed categories, and ushering in new expressions of racial division and oppression, whether hidden or overt. As one thinker summarized this dilemma: "One must weigh reifying vacuous categories whose logic stems from a history of dehumanization against the ability to identify racism, and weigh the sloppiness of racial categories against supporting pundits and politicians who promote a so-called color-blind society that rolls back important strides" (Baker 227).[27]

26   See for example "Racial Measurement in the American Census: Past Practices and Implications for the Future", by C. Matthew Snipp. Also see "Racial Classification in America: Where Do We Go from Here?", by Kenneth Prewitt. Recent changes to the US census, which now presents seven racial/ethnic categories after removing those from the Middle East and North Africa from the category of white, can be found in Rachel Marks et al., "What Updates to OMB's Race/Ethnicity Standards Mean for the Census Bureau." Of course, in the current system, gathering statistics about race, including through the census, is a means for determining how to allocate political and economic power, and for trying to ensure that the aims of programs implemented for equal education or racial justice are effective. Yet, such approaches can be seen as a means for maintaining a racialized society and even an obstacle to consideration of alternative approaches to overcoming discrimination.

27   A dichotomy of colorblindness and essentialism offers a seductive "either-or"; if one approach is correct, the other must be wrong. Bahá'ís should seek to transcend this dichotomy to read reality as accurately as possible and discern when a particular argument or approach may be useful, when it is harmful, and when it may offer partial insights into pressing matters. Because the dichotomy of colorblindness and essentialism is too often exploited by those seeking to ignore or maintain the existing oppressive racialized hierarchy in the United States, it may be difficult to grasp the depths of this dilemma and the way it might stand in the way of achieving unity of thought and action among all fair-minded people who desire to eliminate racial prejudice and discrimination. A few examples may be helpful. Consider, for example, when the practice of Black History Month might be a productive response to the general

Despite the challenge of navigating the tensions between these two perspectives, it is, perhaps, also possible to transcend the apparent dichotomy. "We're at a threshold," one thinker concludes. "We can continue to practice antiracism or promote colorblindness—same coin, different sides—the same ways that we've always done, which will cause us to stay in the matrix and enable race/ism. Or we can forge a new path forward for all of us, one that centers unification, healing, and reconciliation. To create a future without race/ism, we need a way of seeing that will allow us to uncover more of what is concealed and hidden by 'race,' while acknowledging that no one lens alone will ever be completely able to capture our full humanity" (Mason 198). Here, she explains, "race" is a construct that conflates many things—"culture, ethnicity, social class, economic class, the causes/ effects of racism, or some combination thereof" (37)—and by unpacking language and discussing the specific component under consideration apart from its conflation with race, racial ideologies are exposed, and the effects of racism can be understood and addressed without reifying race. In this way, every people can be seen as fully human rather than reduced to a category within a racial hierarchy.

Culture and ethnicity are surely effective and elastic instruments for addressing the beauty and value of human diversity without resort to race. In the United States, diversity has been considered

---

practice of ignoring the contributions of all peoples to American history to American history in schools and textbooks, as opposed to when continuation of such a practice might obstruct necessary progress. See, for example, Michael E. Ross, "Black History Month: Has It Run Its Course?" Another example is the discussion of whether it would be better to prohibit the government from considering matters of race or whether government should be concerned with insuring equal protection before the law, including the formulation of the Fourteenth Amendment and later civil rights legislation. See Coleman Hughes, *The End of Race Politics*, chapter 2. Yet another example is the perspective on literary studies and Black literature. See Sheena Michele Mason, *The Raceless Antiracist*, chapters 2–5. And finally, the issue arises in considering the contribution of academics in the field of philosophy who are Black. See Naomi Zack, *Philosophy of Race*, especially chapter 10. How are such issues to be consistently navigated in the decades ahead—perhaps in different ways in different contexts—along a course that is to ultimately achieve the complete elimination of racial prejudice, without ignoring real problems of racism that exist along the way or selecting approaches that inadvertently crystalize racial division?

from a racialized perspective for so long that the way in which racial categories suppress human diversity has often been obscured. In fact, very different peoples are homogenized by assigning and assimilating them into a few strictly defined racial categories.[28] For example, the 2020 census specifically mentions the following ethnicities, with space to list others, under the single category of an imagined Asian "race": Chinese, Japanese, Indian, Filipino, Vietnamese, Korean, Pakistani and Hmong. What is the point of such a designation, other than to squeeze the ever-increasing diversity of peoples living in the United States into a preexisting racialized system? Surely, such a single, artificial, racial category would be judged to be incoherent, first and foremost, by the many peoples of the Asian continent.

Yet, in a society that favors conflict as a methodology for achieving both intellectual progress and social change, the call to transcend the dichotomized views of race described above may itself risk becoming another position to be argued over. And the stakes of irresoluble debate on these questions are high: the inability to advance towards collective agreement on the definition of the problem contributes to the inability to remedy it in a systematic and an empirical way. Although some in the wider society may claim to have achieved a colorblind social reality, racial disparity nonetheless persists, taking its daily personal toll and maintaining the societal divide. As a result of the perpetual clash of ideas, any advance in one generation is resisted or overturned in the next. Individuals embrace a set of ideas, then use them to fight against others.

Again, it should be noted that the brief discussion offered here cannot fully capture the entire range of discourse on race prevalent in American society. Different individuals, even different Bahá'ís, will have different readings of this reality. The intention here is to illustrate the importance of a continuing reading of reality to inform an evolving framework for action. It is easy to see dichotomies when they are presented in an extreme form. But it is important to realize that both fair-minded Black and white people fall on both sides of this dichotomy between race neutrality and race consciousness, in various ways. And the contrasting responses find expression in various approaches in the political, religious, economic, and social life of the American people.

---

28   See note 26 above.

Addressing these fundamental dilemmas surrounding race has been a central aspect of the work of the Bahá'í Office of Public Affairs in the United States, which provided a description of the problem and proposed a way forward in an unpublished article:

> There is a kind of catch-22 in the current dilemma surrounding the question of racial identity in the United States. As a society, we cannot currently be one people who are "color-blind" and do not see race in a society where racism is a disruptive everyday social force. But, at the same time, if we crystalize race into fixed categories that we each inhabit, we inadvertently reinforce the contemporary racist system. The way forward thus involves reframing identity and purpose reflecting the oneness of humanity, restructuring relationships, building environments of empowerment free of oppression, elevating consciousness, implementing a system of learning based on a pattern of action and reflection, building the capacity of many people to engage in social transformation, raising diverse and integrated communities, and creating new institutions that recognize the potential of every individual and seek to release it. In reality, humanity is searching desperately for a pattern of life to which it can aspire, and racial justice is an integral component of this new way of life. We cannot deal with issues of racism completely apart from or as a precondition to pursuing other vital aspects of the well-being of all.

A few points arise from this reading of reality that inform our emerging framework for action. First, to the extent possible, Bahá'ís should become adept at differentiating between approaches to race that are intended to maintain the existing racial hierarchy and those that, while possibly limited in effectiveness or poorly thought out, are nevertheless well intentioned. It is vital not to bring ill-intended debates into community building efforts, especially those that feed into, or on, the type of contest and politicization that is prevalent in society at this time. Beyond this, a wide range of efforts is possible at the early stage when experiences of proven effectiveness are not yet readily evident. In certain circumstances, a race neutral approach to resolving a

problem may be necessary; under other conditions, a race conscious approach may be required. But these are questions of a
pragmatic orientation toward reality, not of ideology. At its heart,
Bahá'ís understand this dilemma as a tension between oneness
and diversity. Like other dichotomies, rather than becoming
trapped in the contending sides of an intractable "either-or," an
approach to transcending it can be sought. While seeing with the
eye of oneness, the destructive consequences of a racialized society can be identified and addressed; while acknowledging and
valuing diversity, an ill-suited, restrictive categorization of portions of humanity can be avoided. It would seem to be particularly
useful in this respect to be clear about the subject under discussion—such as ethnicity, culture, social policy, or even effects of
racism itself—rather than conflating different issues under the
subject of race; this would assist in analyzing various issues from
a perspective of oneness in light of Bahá'u'lláh's teachings, rather
than perceiving them as a clash among racial groups.

Of course, a distinctive Bahá'í contribution to the issue of race
and racial prejudice consists of more than simply a well-considered approach to navigating the challenges present in the prevailing discourse. An evolving framework for action on this issue will
also incorporate insights from the teachings of the Faith and the
accumulated practical experience of the community. It is to these
that we now turn.

Distinctive Characteristics
of a Bahá'í Approach

IN ADDITION TO A READING OF THE CURRENT SOCIAL REALITY, A
framework for action for the elimination of racial prejudice incor-
porates an appreciation of the Bahá'í vision of the society toward
which we aspire and of the approach to achieve this end.

Liberal societies generally refrain, out of respect for pluralism, from an attempt to describe what is good—the good life
or the common good—leaving the choice of the kind of "good"
to pursue to the personal preferences of individuals. Utility, not
the good, is their professed aim. As a result, when public policy
touches on issues about which there are conflicting opinions, a

contest among contending positions emerges that may extend to a clash of beliefs, values, methods, and even identity. So long as there is an overarching narrative and basis for shared community, some accommodation can be achieved that facilitates common understanding and action. The civil rights movement of the 1960s represented a moment when social consensus in the United States changed, and overt expressions of racial prejudice and white supremacy were increasingly deemed unacceptable in many parts of society. Yet, when such consensus erodes, the contest of values and practices reemerges, and social gains may be rolled up or suppressed by alternative measures. Destructive divisions between "us and them" come to the fore once more. As the Universal House of Justice observed when assessing conditions in the United States: "Sadly, however, your nation's history reveals that any significant progress toward racial equality has invariably been met by countervailing processes, overt or covert, that served to undermine the advances achieved and to reconstitute the forces of oppression by other means" (*Messages 2001–2022* ¶ 374.2). The resulting contest of beliefs and approaches, sometimes even among those who would seem to hold the same ultimate aspirations, detracts from the attention that needs to be directed toward creating new relationships among people—relationships that are based on the principle of the oneness of humanity.

In attempting to understand the Bahá'í approach to the question of the elimination of racial prejudice in America, it is important to keep in mind that no one knows how to achieve this end. The problem has developed and evolved across different manifestations over four centuries. Therefore, it is not a matter of taking any of the existing contemporary perspectives or practices—for example antiracism—and expecting that it will fully resolve the problem.

Nevertheless, as noted above, there are many valuable insights from thinkers within the wider society, and thus, reading the reality of society and understanding the way in which the problem is being approached by various individuals and organizations is an important aspect of the Bahá'í endeavor to work within an evolving framework for action. This, for example, has been a significant component of the work of the National Assembly's Office of Public Affairs in formulating its engagement in the national discourse on race. And of course, all such insights should be weighed in the light of Bahá'u'lláh's teachings and incorporated, as found helpful, in a manner that corresponds with Bahá'í concepts and principles. Bahá'ís might legitimately hold different opinions about the value of various ideas propounded by those who are not Bahá'ís, but they do not allow the profound disagreements and conflicts in wider society to infiltrate the Bahá'í community out of inflexible certainty in a particular diagnosis of a racial problem or a particular prescription propounded in popular culture. Ultimately, Bahá'ís are united by the concepts and approaches presented in the writings of Bahá'u'lláh, 'Abdu'l-Bahá, Shoghi Effendi, and the Universal House of Justice.

Generally, in the wider society, the effort to address concerns associated with race involves diagnosing the various expressions of racism or racial prejudice, and then attempting to fight these expressions through social activism and civic policy prescriptions. This is perfectly understandable and has resulted in many prominent achievements—achievements that are currently under threat by countervailing forces. Yet, the distinctive character of the Bahá'í approach is that it is not centered so much on fighting racism as it is on building a social order that manifests oneness, love and fellowship, unity in diversity, and justice—a social order in which racism finds no place. As a letter written on behalf of the House of Justice explained many years ago:

> Bahá'ís are often accused of holding aloof from the "real problems" of their fellowmen. But when we hear this accusation let us not forget that those who make it are usually idealistic materialists to whom material good is the only "real" good, whereas we know that the working of the material world is merely a reflection of spiritual conditions and until the spiritual conditions can be changed there can be no lasting change for the better in material affairs.
>
> We should also remember that most people have no clear concept of the sort of world they wish to build, nor how to go about building it. Even those who are concerned to improve conditions are therefore reduced to combating every apparent evil that takes their attention. Willingness to fight against evils, whether in the form of conditions or

embodied in evil men, has thus become for most people the touchstone by which they judge a person's moral worth. Bahá'ís, on the other hand, know the goal they are working towards and know what they must do, step by step, to attain it. Their whole energy is directed towards the building of the good, a good which has such a positive strength that in the face of it the multitude of evils—which are in essence negative—will fade away and be no more. To enter into the quixotic tournament of demolishing one by one the evils in the world is, to a Bahá'í, a vain waste of time and effort. His whole life is directed towards proclaiming the Message of Bahá'u'lláh, reviving the spiritual life of his fellowmen, uniting them in a divinely-created World Order, and then, as the Order grows in strength and influence, he will see the power of that Message transforming the whole human society and progressively solving the problems and removing the injustices which have so long bedeviled the world. (*Messages 1963-1986* ¶ 173.11c–d)

Shoghi Effendi explains that the plan that Bahá'u'lláh has given us may not conform to the perspectives and proposals of human beings:

And as we make an effort to demonstrate that love to the world may we also clear our minds of any lingering trace of unhappy misunderstandings that might obscure our clear conception of the exact purpose and methods of this new world order, so challenging and complex, yet so consummate and wise. We are called upon by our beloved Master in His Will and Testament not only to adopt it unreservedly, but to unveil its merit to all the world. To attempt to estimate its full value, and grasp its exact significance after so short a time since its inception would be premature and presumptuous on our part. We must trust to time, and the guidance of God's Universal House of Justice, to obtain a clearer and fuller understanding of its provisions and implications. But one word of warning must be uttered in this connection. Let us be on our guard lest we measure too strictly the Divine Plan with the standard of men. I am not prepared to state that it agrees in principle or in method with the prevailing notions now uppermost in men's minds, nor that it should conform with those imperfect, precarious, and expedient measures feverishly resorted to by agitated humanity. Are we to doubt that the ways of God are not necessarily the ways of man? Is not faith but another word for implicit obedience, whole-hearted allegiance, uncompromising adherence to that which we believe is the revealed and express will of God, however perplexing it might first appear, however at variance with the shadowy views, the impotent doctrines, the crude theories, the idle imaginings, the fashionable conceptions of a transient and troublous age? If we are to falter or hesitate, if our love for Him should fail to direct us and keep us within His path, if we desert Divine and emphatic principles, what hope can we any more cherish for healing the ills and sicknesses of this world? (*Bahá'í Administration* 62)

A Bahá'í approach to social change, then, eschews "the quixotic tournament of demolishing one by one the evils in the world," and focuses on the construction of a new social order. From a Bahá'í perspective, for humanity to learn how to rise above the intractable dilemma on race requires the recognition of the spiritual truth of the oneness of humanity that must be made manifest in a social order of unity in diversity. It must now be determined how to move from this ontological truth to the achievement of this just end.

That is, biologically and spiritually, the human race is one; now a new social reality must be constructed based on this proper understanding of human nature. We must recognize that we are all human beings, we all share a common twofold moral purpose to develop a noble character and to find some way to act in service to humanity, and therefore we all have the right to exercise our God-given powers of mind, heart, spirit, volition, and agency. Justice requires that all live free of social discrimination and barriers that allow the oppression and exploitation of some part of humanity for the advantage of another part. At the same time, we have to recognize the rich tapestry of the diversity of the human race that has, historically, given rise to different peoples and cultures, each with their own values and achievements, and each of which can and must contribute its distinctive and constructive share to the building of unified nations, and a unified world. In this respect, each culture has its merits and its shortcomings, and it is up to each people to weigh its culture to determine what gifts it has to offer to all humanity, and which dark tendencies it must weed out to respect the principle of the oneness of humanity and to contribute to the betterment of the world.

In learning how to act in a manner that is systematic and grows in complexity over time, Bahá'ís strive to understand how to move from where we are to where we are going—toward a future where racial prejudice has been eliminated. While it is impossible to fully see the end at the beginning, it is possible to see progress to a certain extent—the next horizon of understanding and action—and then work toward it until another new horizon opens. Insights can be drawn from thoughtful individuals both inside and outside the community, without becoming ensnared in the catch-22 of colorblindness and essentialism, by weighing perspectives in the light of the Bahá'í teachings and practical experience over time. In this way, it is possible to see with the eye of oneness, without being blind to the manifestations of a racialized social reality that require a corrective response. We begin to create this new reality in the small social spaces currently available and systematically increase the number and the reach of those spaces. Over time, understanding and practice can continually evolve to achieve a future society reshaped according to the understanding that humanity is one. In such a society, decisions pertaining to social, economic, and political life will not allow one part of the human race to be suppressed, subordinated, or exploited for the benefit of others. Ultimately, the social construct of a racialized hierarchy that emerged to oppress portions of humanity will be set aside.

"God," 'Abdu'l-Bahá declares, "maketh no distinction between the white and the black." "God did not make these divisions," He affirms, "these divisions have had their origin in man himself. Therefore, as they are against the plan and purpose of God they are false and imaginary" (qtd. in Shoghi Effendi, *Advent* 37). And again: "Variations of color, of land and of race are of no importance in the Bahá'í Faith; on the contrary, Bahá'í unity overcometh them all and doeth away with all these fancies and imaginations" (*Selections* 112). "Strive jointly to make extraordinary progress and mix together completely," 'Abdu'l-Bahá urges. "I pray that you attain to such a degree of good character and behavior that the names of black and white shall vanish. All shall be called human" (*Promulgation* 46). And He adds: "When the racial elements of the American nation unite in actual fellowship and accord, the lights of the oneness of humanity will shine, the day of eternal glory and bliss will dawn, the spirit of God encompass, and the divine favors descend" (56). "Love and unity will be fostered between you, thereby bringing about the oneness of mankind. For the accomplishment of unity . . . will be an assurance of the world's peace. Then racial prejudice, national prejudice, limited patriotism and religious bias will pass away and remain no longer" (*Bahá'í World Faith* 269).

These expressions of 'Abdu'l-Bahá may be seen as the highest aspiration of those who hold, with sincerity and fairmindedness, to perspectives of either colorblindness or essentialism: the complete extinction of any conception or manifestation of prejudice of race. For the United States, this means the malign conception of race formulated in countless permutations across four centuries to dehumanize and oppress, will be displaced by a new conception of people who are united and diverse, in a way that today cannot be fully conceived.

Thus, from the Bahá'í perspective, the elimination of racial prejudice is not to be achieved through the clash of differing belief systems, of conceptions of identity, of sets of values, or of prescriptions for particular solutions. It will emerge through the investigation of truth and the pursuit of the common good—the shared effort to aim toward the set of authentic relationships that result in human flourishing, individually and collectively, in which no one is considered to be "other," and none are oppressed for the benefit of others. From small rural villages to the international arena of the United Nations, Bahá'ís are striving with increasing success to bring people together in unity and common purpose to search for solutions to the challenges facing humanity.

Some Relevant Insights
from the Teachings of Bahá'u'lláh

A framework for action that is consciously extended to address the challenge of the elimination of racial prejudice will naturally encompass within it the fundamental elements already included in the work underway for the current series of stages of the unfoldment of the Divine Plan. This includes concepts, methods, and instruments such as operating in a learning mode involving study, consultation, action, and reflection; capacity building and the institute process; beginning activities simply and evolving in complexity over time; the nature of the desired relationships among individuals, communities and institutions; spiritual and material education that extends from childhood to maturity; and coherence between community building, social action, and involvement in the discourses of society. To these must be added those elements from the Bahá'í teachings and the experience of the community that specifically pertain to combatting racial prejudice and to setting out the way forward to attain its ultimate extirpation from the life of society. Of the many relevant elements, the following are among the most important.

THE PRINCIPLE OF THE ONENESS OF HUMANITY

Of course, the central teaching of Bahá'u'lláh is the oneness of humanity. Bahá'u'lláh unequivocally states that all human beings are one and, for the first time in human history, has affirmed that there is no justification for the division of human beings into different categories of "us" and "them" that has characterized every society and every stage of social organization to the present day. "Verily, the words which have descended from the heaven of the Will of God are the source of unity and harmony for the world," He explains. "Close your eyes to racial differences, and welcome all with the light of oneness" (qtd. in Shoghi Effendi, *Advent* 37). 'Abdu'l-Bahá captures this fundamental transformation in one of His talks:

The teachings specialized in Bahá'u'lláh are addressed to humanity. He says, "Ye are all the leaves of one tree." He does not say, "Ye are the leaves of two trees: one divine, the other satanic." He has declared that each individual member of the human family is a leaf or branch upon the Adamic tree; that all are sheltered beneath the protecting mercy and providence of God; that all are the children of God, fruit upon the one tree of His love. God is equally compassionate and kind to all the leaves, branches and fruit of this tree. Therefore, there is no satanic tree whatever—Satan being a product of human minds and of instinctive human tendencies toward error. God alone is Creator, and all are creatures of His might. Therefore, we must love mankind as His creatures, realizing that all are growing upon the tree of His mercy, servants of His omnipotent will and manifestations of His good pleasure. (*Promulgation* 230–31)

Thus, for Bahá'ís the essential nature of all human beings is the same. Every human being is endowed by the Creator with a soul possessing inherent powers. Each person shares the same purpose. Each should be respected for this common divine endowment, and there can be no spiritual, moral or social justification for the oppression and exploitation of some for the benefit of others. Each person is a trust of society, and each must be safeguarded and empowered so that these latent potentialities can be revealed.

However, it is not enough that this principle of the oneness of humanity merely be acknowledged. A new social order must be forged based on its full embrace and ultimate expression. All human relationships are to be recast in the light of the principle of the oneness of humanity. This requires the elimination of all forms of prejudice—including specifically racial prejudice—that have served as humanity's practical mechanisms for justifying otherness. This new order will represent the consummation of millennia of human social evolution. As Shoghi Effendi explains:

Let there be no mistake. The principle of the Oneness of Mankind—the pivot round which all the teachings of Bahá'u'lláh revolve—is no mere outburst of ignorant emotionalism or an expression of vague and pious hope. Its appeal is not to be merely identified with a reawakening of the spirit of brotherhood and good-will among men, nor does it aim solely at the fostering of harmonious coopera- tion among individual peoples and nations. Its implications are deeper, its claims greater than any which the Prophets of old were allowed to advance. Its message is applicable not only to the individual, but concerns itself primarily with the nature of those essential relationships that must bind all the states and nations as members of one human family. It does not constitute merely the enunciation of an ideal, but stands inseparably associated with an institution adequate to embody its truth, demonstrate its validity, and perpetuate its influence. It implies an organic change in the structure of present-day society, a change such as the world has not yet experienced. . . .

It represents the consummation of human evolution— an evolution that has had its earliest beginnings in the birth of family life, its subsequent development in the achieve- ment of tribal solidarity, leading in turn to the constitution of the city-state, and expanding later into the institution of independent and sovereign nations. (*World Order* 42–43)

ONENESS EXPRESSED AS UNITY IN DIVERSITY

The concept of oneness, in the Bahá'í teachings, however, does not mean sameness or uniformity. The reality of oneness is to be manifested in the world by a social order of unity in diversity, as explained by 'Abdu'l-Bahá:

Consider the flowers of a garden. Though differing in kind, color, form, and shape, yet, inasmuch as they are refreshed by the waters of one spring, revived by the breath of one wind, invigorated by the rays of one sun, this diversity in- creaseth their charm, and addeth unto their beauty. How un- pleasing to the eye if all the flowers and plants, the leaves and blossoms, the fruits, the branches and the trees of that garden were all of the same shape and color! Diversity of hues, form and shape, enricheth and adorneth the garden, and heighteneth the effect thereof. In like manner, when divers shades of thought, temperament and character, are brought together under the power and influence of one central agency, the beauty and glory of human perfection will be revealed and made manifest. . . .

Hence the intention must be purified, the effort ennobled and exalted, so that you may establish affinity between the hearts of the world of humanity. (*Tablets* ¶¶ 14.7, 14.59)

Although human beings are one, diversity derives from the lived experience of peoples over time. These varied experiences give rise to cultures that contain both positive and negative characteristics that are intertwined. In this process, humanity has divided itself based on religious, nationalistic, economic, racial, and other forms of prejudice and otherness. In this way, racism and race became manifest in the contemporary social order in the United States. Resolving the matter is not merely a process of reconstructing a racialized social reality into another form; it is about creating a social reality in which—while diversity will exist in a form which perhaps we cannot even currently conceive—racial hierarchies have no part. In the effort to establish a united global spiritual and material civilization, divisiveness and oppressive practices have to be overcome in every nation and among every people.

This process of reflection and change is already underway in Bahá'í communities everywhere. In *The Advent of Divine Justice*, Shoghi Effendi called upon the American Bahá'ís over a century ago to begin to "to weed out, by every means in their power, those faults, habits, and tendencies which they have inherited from their own nation, and to cultivate, patiently and prayerfully, those distinctive qualities and characteristics that are so indispensable to their effective participation in the great redemptive work of their Faith" (20). Recently, the Universal House of Justice wrote to the Bahá'ís in the Democratic Republic of the Congo:

Each culture has many salutary elements that are conducive to promoting unity in diversity, which must be reinforced, as well as negative aspects that contribute to breeding prejudice, which must be gradually abandoned. Meaningful interactions among people hailing from different human groups foster an environment within which advances in culture can occur. To retain and promote customs and traditions that generate animosity is a grave obstacle to the betterment of society. A Bahá'í community is robbed of its ability to promote unity in diversity if the friends, knowingly or unknowingly, reproduce in their interactions and their association with society the same tendencies that foment prejudice. (1 November 2022)

A COMMON IDENTITY

It is difficult to imagine an American society where racism and racial prejudice find no place. How will people conceive of themselves in a nation where the oneness of the citizenry finds expression in unity in diversity without anyone being considered as "other"? One of the advantages of an evolving conceptual framework is that it is possible to begin to walk a path of social change even if the final destination cannot be fully elaborated.

For Bahá'ís, a great advantage in this regard is a shared identity, borne of becoming a Bahá'í, that already transcends race and otherness. Naturally, Bahá'ís do not immediately shed the negative influences of their society upon recognizing Bahá'u'lláh, but His teachings do provide them will the full vision of what it means to be a Bahá'í, to which they aspire and towards which they work day by day. It is in this context that Shoghi Effendi describes Bahá'ís of the current period as "the 'generation of the half-light,' living at a time which may be designated as the period of the incubation of the World Commonwealth envisaged by Bahá'u'lláh" (*World Order* 168). Our shared identity as Bahá'ís, however tenuously expressed in this transitional period, creates an opportunity for rising together above the prejudices and crystallized divisions of humanity to see ourselves as one, and as one family, address any problems that arise from the challenges introduced by the wider society. We then serve as a leaven to assist all peoples to perceive themselves as one. As 'Abdu'l-Bahá explains:

You must become of one heart, one spirit and one susceptibility. May you become as the waves of one sea, stars of the

same heaven, fruits adorning the same tree, roses of one garden in order that through you the oneness of humanity may
establish its temple in the world of mankind, for you are the
ones who are called to uplift the cause of unity among the
nations of the earth. (*Promulgation* 214)

Amongst Bahá'ís, then, there need never be the contest among
ideas and values of defined, so-called racial categories—whether
White, Black, Asian, Hispanic, American Indian, Pacific Islander,
or Middle Eastern. The ensigns of diversity cannot become the
cause of difference within the Bahá'í community-building efforts
underway. As 'Abdu'l-Bahá envisions the coming change:

Whensoever holy souls, drawing on the powers of heaven,
shall arise with such qualities of the spirit, and march in
unison, rank on rank, every one of those souls will be even
as one thousand, and the surging waves of that mighty ocean
will be even as the battalions of the Concourse on high. What
a blessing that will be—when all shall come together, even
as once separate torrents, rivers and streams, running brooks
and single drops, when collected together in one place will
form a mighty sea. And to such a degree will the inherent
unity of all prevail, that the traditions, rules, customs and
distinctions in the fanciful life of these populations will be
effaced and vanish away like isolated drops, once the great
sea of oneness doth leap and surge and roll. . . .

O ye loved ones of God! Struggle and strive to reach
that high station, and to make a splendor so to shine across
these realms of earth that the rays of it will be reflected back
from a dawning-point on the horizon of eternity. This is the
very foundation of the Cause of God. This is the very pith of
the Law of God. This is the mighty structure raised up by the
Manifestations of God. This is why the orb of God's world
dawneth. This is why the Lord establisheth Himself on the
throne of His human body. (*Selections* 260)

It is evident from statements of 'Abdu'l-Bahá that, from the
Bahá'í perspective, diversity is not concerned with difference
of type, but with the valuable variety of things that are of the

same type. "The garden is more beautiful when the flowers are many-colored and different; the variety lends charm and adornment," He states. "In a flock of doves some are white, some black, red, blue; yet they make no distinction among themselves. All are doves no matter what the color. This variety in forms and colorings which is manifest in all the kingdoms is according to creative wisdom and has a divine purpose" (*Promulgation* 112–13).

JUSTICE IS MANIFESTED BY ESTABLISHING PROPER RELATIONSHIPS

The perspective that the oneness of humanity must be consciously understood and find expression in a social order that manifests unity in diversity makes it evident that racial problems are problems of relationships. Often, however, racism and racial prejudice are framed as problems of belief, to be addressed by the adoption of a particular set of ideas, or a full ideology that is held to be true and by which questions of race must be measured. The problem with such competing ideological claims is that the contest between them continues interminably.[29]

Bahá'ís see the matter differently. To be a Bahá'í is not to be a true believer in a world of "infidels," or to hold to a correct set of theological concepts or moral doctrines that are in contest with others. "Religion," 'Abdu'l-Bahá explains, "is not a series of beliefs, a set of customs; religion is the teachings of the Lord God, teachings which constitute the very life of humankind, which urge high thoughts upon the mind, refine the character, and lay the groundwork for man's everlasting honor" (*Selections* 52). Thus, Bahá'ís do not argue about or seek to compel the adoption of a particular set of ideas—whether about race or anything else. Rather, Bahá'u'lláh explains that, "[t]heir concern hath ever been and now is for the betterment of the world. Their purpose is to obliterate differences, and quench the flame of hatred and enmity, so that the whole earth may come to be viewed as one country" (*Epistle* 122).

---

29   For an exploration of the problem of ideology, which holds certain beliefs to be of greater value than a human being, and thereby obstructs the establishment of just and moral relationships, see William S. Hatcher, *Love, Power and Justice*.

Bahá'u'lláh states that justice "consisteth in rendering each his due" (*Tabernacle* ¶ 2.37), and that the "purpose of justice is the appearance of unity among men" (*Tablets* 66). For Bahá'ís, the social order is in a state of disintegration because the way human beings are associated with one another is inadequate for the current requirements of a world that has effectively shrunk into a single neighborhood. The fate of all peoples is now inextricably bound together. The manner of association of past ages, the prejudices and practices that enabled people to oppress and advance themselves over others, are entirely unsuited to humanity's current condition. Thus 'Abdu'l-Bahá explains:

> The morals of humanity must undergo change. New remedies and solutions for human problems must be adopted. Human intellects themselves must change and be subject to the universal reformation. Just as the thoughts and hypotheses of past ages are fruitless today, likewise dogmas and codes of human invention are obsolete and barren of product in religion. . . . Therefore, it is our duty in this radiant century to investigate the essentials of divine religion, seek the realities underlying the oneness of the world of humanity and discover the source of fellowship and agreement which will unite mankind in the heavenly bond of love. (*Promulgation* 144)

Thus, the aim of Bahá'ís is to learn to establish such just relationships in the world among individuals, communities, and institutions, to heal the differences that have divided humanity, and to contribute to the emergence of a new social order that serves the well-being of all. 'Abdu'l-Bahá states that they must "strive with all their might until universal fellowship, close and warm, and unalloyed love, and spiritual relationships, will connect all the hearts in the world" (*Selections* 21).

Just Relationships Depend on the Expression of Spiritual Qualities

The challenge of building unity, of creating a society in which racial prejudice finds no place, is immeasurably more difficult than protesting about the existence of racial prejudice, of fighting against its various manifestations, or of criticizing individuals or institutions that fall short in some way. Elimination of racial prejudice requires the establishment of just relationships among individuals, the community, and institutions. And the establishment of just relationships depends on the cultivation and expression of spiritual qualities. Consider, for instance, this vivid description of the example of 'Abdu'l-Bahá cited by Shoghi Effendi:

> Let them call to mind, fearlessly and determinedly, the example and conduct of 'Abdu'l-Bahá while in their midst. Let them remember His courage, His genuine love, His informal and indiscriminating fellowship, His contempt for and impatience of criticism, tempered by His tact and wisdom. Let them revive and perpetuate the memory of those unforgettable and historic episodes and occasions on which He so strikingly demonstrated His keen sense of justice, His spontaneous sympathy for the downtrodden, His ever-abiding sense of the oneness of the human race, His overflowing love for its members, and His displeasure with those who dared to flout His wishes, to deride His methods, to challenge His principles, or to nullify His acts. (*Advent* 34)

In the various paragraphs of his argument in *The Advent of Divine Justice*, Shoghi Effendi returns again and again to the spiritual qualities required for so substantial a transformation in American society as to efface this long standing and deeply rooted evil, sometimes offering insights from 'Abdu'l-Bahá and sometimes presenting his own. The task requires "spiritual love and heavenly harmony," "perfect love, unity and kindness," "faith, assurance, and the teachings of the Blessed Beauty" (39), as well as "extreme patience, true humility, consummate tact, sound initiative, mature wisdom, and deliberate, persistent, and prayerful effort" (40). These are but a few of the many qualities called for in the Bahá'í teachings to address the challenge of establishing just relationships for a new age of human maturity.

SHARED RESPONSIBILITY

Once it becomes evident that the aim of the elimination of racial prejudice is the establishment of just and unifying relationships among people who possess the same essential nature and purpose, it is then indisputable that the resolution of the problem is a matter of mutual responsibilities. For it is not possible for one party to be responsible for a relationship among equals. While the current debate in society often takes the form of a false dichotomy between white or Black responsibility to resolve the lingering impacts of racial prejudice, more than a century ago 'Abdu'l-Bahá emphasized the shared nature of this challenge for all Bahá'ís:

> Strive earnestly and put forth your greatest endeavor toward the accomplishment of this fellowship and the cementing of this bond of brotherhood between you. Such an attainment is not possible without will and effort on the part of each. . . . Each one should endeavor to develop and assist the other toward mutual advancement. . . . Love and unity will be fostered between you, thereby bringing about the oneness of mankind. (qtd. in Shoghi Effendi, *Advent* 39)

Shoghi Effendi similarly emphasizes mutual responsibility in *The Advent of Divine Justice.* "A tremendous effort is required by both races if their outlook, their manners, and conduct are to reflect, in this darkened age, the spirit and teachings of the Faith of Bahá'u'lláh," he explains. "Casting away once and for all the fallacious doctrine of racial superiority, with its attendant evils, confusion, and miseries, and welcoming and encouraging the intermixture of races, and tearing down the barriers that now divide them, they should each endeavor, day and night, to fulfill their particular responsibilities in the common task which so urgently faces them." All believers, he indicated, are to "participate in, and lend their assistance, each according to his or her capacity, experience, and opportunities, to the common task of fulfilling the instructions, realizing the hopes, and following the example, of 'Abdu'l-Bahá." To none, he further asserted, is given the right to "be regarded as absolved from such an obligation" (51). And he adds:

Let neither think that the solution of so vast a problem is a matter that exclusively concerns the other. Let neither think that such a problem can either easily or immediately be resolved. Let neither think that they can wait confidently for the solution of this problem until the initiative has been taken, and the favorable circumstances created, by agencies that stand outside the orbit of their Faith. . . . Let them rather believe, and be firmly convinced, that on their mutual understanding, their amity, and sustained cooperation, must depend, more than on any other force or organization operating outside the circle of their Faith, the deflection of that dangerous course so greatly feared by 'Abdu'l-Bahá, and the materialization of the hopes He cherished for their joint contribution to the fulfillment of that country's glorious destiny. (*Advent* 40–41)

The fact that there is a shared responsibility does not mean that the responsibility is identical in all its expressions, as passages in the Bahá'í writings make evident. For example, Shoghi Effendi states:

Let the white make a supreme effort in their resolve to contribute their share to the solution of this problem, to abandon once for all their usually inherent and at times subconscious sense of superiority, to correct their tendency towards revealing a patronizing attitude towards the members of the other race, to persuade them through their intimate, spontaneous and informal association with them of the genuineness of their friendship and the sincerity of their intentions, and to master their impatience of any lack of responsiveness on the part of a people who have received, for so long a period, such grievous and slow-healing wounds. Let the Negroes, through a corresponding effort on their part, show by every means in their power the warmth of their response, their readiness to forget the past, and their ability to wipe out every trace of suspicion that may still linger in their hearts and minds. (*Advent* 40)

In this regard, the House of Justice has praised the constructive resilience of Bahá'ís "who have labored so persistently to promote race unity, especially the African American friends" (4 February 2018). The endless permutations of racial obstacles thrown up by a society resistant to justice and change, and the sometimes slow response of the Bahá'í community itself, at times requires Bahá'ís who are Black to call upon deeper levels of patience and persistence. Meanwhile, because the form that racialization takes in the United States makes it possible for Bahá'ís who are white to remain largely unconscious of, or apathetic to, the expressions of racial prejudice in their society, it is incumbent upon these friends to see themselves as protagonists in a process of reading their reality to understand how these racial forces operate, and to learn to contribute to overcoming them. And so it is for all the friends of whatever background in the ever more diverse contemporary American society. The many requirements of Bahá'í fellowship, including having a sin-covering eye and avoiding criticism, make it impossible for anyone to assume the responsibility for calling out the shortcomings of other individuals, thus underlining the vital necessity of each person consciously assuming the obligations ordained by Bahá'u'lláh and 'Abdu'l-Bahá. "There can be no rest until the desired outcome is achieved," the House of Justice explains (*Messages 2001-2022* ¶ 374.5).

CREATING EVER-LARGER SOCIAL SPACES THAT MANIFEST THE ONENESS OF HUMANITY

The Bahá'í approach to the challenge of racism and racial prejudice is thus not concerned merely with a description and diagnosis of the problems prevalent in society. Nor does it propose some form of engagement in a contest of ideas, values, or approaches—most particularly among those fair-minded people who have different perceptions about the nature of the problem and its resolution. Because its central concern is the absence of proper and just relationships, the Bahá'í response centers on overcoming obstacles and creating new relationships that are characterized by the spiritual qualities described in the Bahá'í writings. Such relationships are based on an appreciation of the oneness of humanity and are manifested as unity in diversity.

This is the same approach to the elimination of racial prejudice that Shoghi Effendi emphasized years earlier. "Incapable as yet, in view of the restricted size of their community and the limited influence it now wields, of producing any marked effect on the great mass of their countrymen," he explains, "let them focus their attention, for the present, on their own selves, their own individual needs, their own personal deficiencies and weaknesses" (*Advent* 20). He then calls upon the Bahá'í community to address those social spaces already within its grasp:

> The consciousness of any division or cleavage in its ranks is alien to its very purpose, principles, and ideals. Once its members have fully recognized the claim of its Author, and, by identifying themselves with its Administrative Order, accepted unreservedly the principles and laws embodied in its teachings, every differentiation of class, creed, or color must automatically be obliterated, and never be allowed, under any pretext, and however great the pressure of events or of public opinion, to reassert itself....
>
> Freedom from racial prejudice, in any of its forms, should, at such a time as this when an increasingly large section of the human race is falling a victim to its devastating ferocity, be adopted as the watchword of the entire body of the American believers, in whichever state they reside, in whatever circles they move, whatever their age, traditions, tastes, and habits. It should be consistently demonstrated in every phase of their activity and life, whether in the Bahá'í community or outside it, in public or in private, formally as well as informally, individually as well as in their official capacity as organized groups, committees and Assemblies. It should be deliberately cultivated through the various and everyday opportunities, no matter how insignificant, that present themselves, whether in their homes, their business offices, their schools and colleges, their social parties and recreation grounds, their Bahá'í meetings, conferences, conventions, summer schools and Assemblies. It should, above all else, become the keynote of the policy of that august body which, in its capacity as the national representative, and the director and coordinator of the affairs of the community,

must set the example, and facilitate the application of such a vital principle to the lives and activities of those whose interests it safeguards and represents. (*Advent* 33–37)

Thus, Shoghi Effendi called for the Bahá'ís to demonstrate freedom from prejudice "in their homes, their business offices, their schools and colleges, their social parties and recreation grounds, their Bahá'í meetings, conferences, conventions, summer schools and Assemblies." The challenge, as he presented it, is not so much about fighting racism in every social space, as it is about building something new in every space in which Bahá'ís are active: sound personal and social relationships based on Bahá'u'lláh's teachings that enable people to work together as equals in a collective process to foster individual and social transformation.

The basic approach of Shoghi Effendi has been expanded by the Universal House of Justice in the context of the recent stages of the Divine Plan to encompass clusters as well as neighborhoods and villages that are centers of intense activity, involving complementary efforts for community building, social action, and involvement in the discourses of society. Every core activity, every neighborhood or cluster activity, every initiative for social action, every discourse, becomes a space where the oneness of humanity is manifested and safeguarded. Each of these social spaces are environments in which a new set of relationships based on spiritual principles and qualities are forged. Each can, over time, grow in size, in complexity, and in their impact on society. Gradually, old, oppressive conceptions of race are deconstructed, and new conceptions of unity in diversity based on the oneness of humanity emerge. A letter written on behalf of the House of Justice states:

Here, the Guardian is calling for the friends to address the question of race unity as a part of life in all of the social spaces in which they are engaged, and, similarly, the House of Justice is now saying that freedom from racial prejudice must be the watchword of Bahá'ís in the social spaces in which they are engaged for the activities of the Plan. In such intimate settings, people of diverse racial backgrounds encounter the Word of God, and in their efforts to translate the

Teachings into practical action, are able to generate bonds of love, affection, and unity, and to learn what it means to establish a true interracial fellowship that is powerful enough to overcome the forces of racism that afflict them and their society. Currently, among the Bahá'ís of the United States, race unity is a dimension of the work of community building in scores of clusters, of social action in hundreds of efforts of various levels of complexity, and of involvement in the discourses of society by thousands of believers in various settings. The House of Justice is confident that these endeavors will become more systematic, more widespread, and more effective as the learning process already set in motion by your National Spiritual Assembly is persistently pursued by the believers in greater numbers. Parallel with this, of course, is the effort of the National Assembly to engage at the national level in the discourse concerning race. In the same way as the other activities of the Plan, every challenge the community faces in the work of race unity will be overcome as capacity is raised among an expanding group of friends in each cluster through learning and systematic action. (6 August 2018)

This brings us, then, from a consideration of the teachings that inform a framework for the elimination of racial prejudice, to a consideration of how the framework is being applied to ever greater effect in the context of the current efforts of the Bahá'í world.

The Nine Year Plan and the Elimination of Racial Prejudice

FOR MORE THAN A DECADE, THE HOUSE OF JUSTICE HAS WRITTEN extensively to the friends in the United States, sometimes to individuals and sometime collectively, about the challenge of racial prejudice afflicting their nation and how to address and ultimately overcome it in the context of the unfoldment of the Divine Plan. As part of this correspondence, the House of Justice emphasized that racial prejudice is not susceptible to remedy merely through a simple course of study, or by adopting the prevalent thoughts and approaches circulating in the wider society:

> Racism is a profound deviation from the standard of true morality. It deprives a portion of humanity of the opportunity to cultivate and express the full range of their capability and to live a meaningful and flourishing life, while blighting the progress of the rest of humankind. It cannot be rooted out by contest and conflict. It must be supplanted by the establishment of just relationships among individuals, communities, and institutions of society that will uplift all and will not designate anyone as "other". The change required is not merely social and economic, but above all moral and spiritual. Within the context of the framework governing your activities, it is necessary to carefully examine the forces unfolding around you to determine where your energies might reinforce the most promising initiatives, what you should avoid, and how you might lend a distinctive contribution. It is not possible for you to effect the transformation envisioned by Bahá'u'lláh merely by adopting the perspectives, practices, concepts, criticisms, and language of contemporary society. Your approach, instead, will be distinguished by maintaining a humble posture of learning, weighing alternatives in the light of His teachings, consulting to harmonize differing views and shape collective action, and marching forward with unbreakable unity in serried lines. (*Messages 2011-2022* ¶ 374.4)

Thus, in place of the kinds of efforts prevalent in the wider society, the House of Justice calls upon the friends to appreciate how the efforts currently underway for the unfoldment of the Divine Plan present the opportunity for them to learn—beginning simply and growing in complexity over time—to eradicate racial prejudice and to create ever larger social spaces governed by racial harmony. In their activities for community building, social action, and involvement in the discourses of society, the friends can work together as one family and build sound relationships free of prejudice, learning to resolve challenges as they arise.

On the issue of racial prejudice and its practical impact as described in your letter, the House of Justice feels that Bahá'ís can best learn to respond to the problem of racial prejudice through their daily effort to apply the teachings of Bahá'u'lláh in their personal lives as well as through their involvement in community-building activities, social action, and the discourses of society. You are therefore encouraged to strive to promote meaningful relationships among people of all races in your community and seek to enrich the conversations in whatever social spaces you participate by drawing on perspectives from the Bahá'í teachings and the experience of the Bahá'í community. Undoubtedly, as the Bahá'í community grows, its capacity to address such issues will correspondingly increase. (19 December 2020)

This approach was elaborated upon in another letter to an individual believer.

At this time, the people of the United States do not have unity of thought and vision about how the problem of racial prejudice can be resolved; they are, instead, divided socially and politically on this issue. As you witness, even among Black intellectuals, as well as within the African American community more generally, there are disparate views. Therefore, rather than becoming enmeshed in patterns of behavior pervasive in the wider society that seek to assign blame or deal with issues at the level of broad generalities, Bahá'ís have the opportunity to address the challenge of racial prejudice through the instrumentality of the teachings of Bahá'u'lláh and His Administrative Order. They do so by concentrating on practical challenges in specific settings through consultation in an atmosphere of love and common purpose.

Every believer can address the improvement of his or her own character. Each can strive to work alongside others to ensure that the social spaces in which they participate—especially in families, local communities, places of work and education, Bahá'í activities, Spiritual Assemblies, and committees—manifest freedom from prejudice in all its forms.

Furthermore, the framework for action of the current Plan enables the believers to expand the reach of these efforts by engaging others in neighborhoods and clusters in the process of community building, initiatives for social action, and the prevalent discourses of society. In these contexts, when a specific concern is identified, the believers and their friends can explore the problem together and then participate in a process of learning how to resolve it, while eschewing any inclination toward withdrawal or conflict. Thus, day by day, in practical ways, they learn to solve particular problems that arise and at the same time build capacity to address more complex issues.

As the friends around the world have adopted this approach to address problems in diverse societies, promising signs are already appearing in many places where the Plan's framework for action has taken root. For example, in the Bihar Sharif cluster in India, the oppressive influence of the centuries-old caste system is gradually being undone at the grassroots. The communities in this cluster are learning to mix without regard to caste, so much so that the friends are visiting the homes of families from different castes. To cite another example, in the Lubumbashi cluster in the Democratic Republic of the Congo, the inequality between the sexes has long prevented women from speaking in the presence of men in various social spaces. Now, however, women have been given the courage to freely share their ideas and consult with men in different settings.

You indicate that you have decided to focus on spreading the Faith among African Americans and to dedicate yourself to their advancement and upliftment. This will, no doubt, allow you to learn how to create a social space for individuals to come together in a new pattern of engagement. The House of Justice hopes that you might find one or two other like-minded believers who can assist you in applying the instruments and methods of the Plan to cultivate a dynamic and growing pattern of community life. In this regard, when reaching out to those from the wider community, you can present the message of Bahá'u'lláh as the healing remedy for the ills of humanity and invite the receptive souls you encounter to become protagonists of a constant effort to learn to apply His teachings effectively, explaining that Bahá'ís are also learning to walk this same path. As 'Abdu'l-Bahá is reported to have remarked: "The earth plane is a workshop, not an art gallery for the exhibits of perfect powers. This is not the plane of perfection, but earth is the crucible for refining and molding character." (15 December 2020)

From this perspective on the efforts unfolding in the context of the Divine Plan, it is possible to avoid another false dichotomy of thought that may arise when reflecting upon the elimination of prejudice. One part of this dichotomy is to believe that nothing can be done in the Bahá'í community until every manifestation of the influence of racial prejudice imposed by the wider society is eliminated; in this light, every effort must, first and foremost, center on the most challenging issue described by the Guardian. The other part suggests that such considerations may be set aside because addressing the Plan will—somehow, in a manner unspecified—resolve the problem by itself. Neither of these approaches would prove practical or efficacious; neither is being proposed. Rather there is a reciprocal interplay between the activities of the Plan and the elimination of racial prejudice. As the capabilities of individuals to translate Bahá'u'lláh's teachings into reality are strengthened, and the community grows and expands its efforts, the ability to engage the challenge of racial prejudice, both in scope and depth, will increase. And the progress that derives from this engagement, from both successes and challenges, will contribute to the greater capacity of the community for growth and social change. The reciprocal relationships of simultaneous individual and social transformation are captured in a letter written on behalf of the Guardian:

We cannot segregate the human heart from the environment outside us and say that once one of these is reformed everything will be improved. Man is organic with the world. His inner life molds the environment and is itself also deeply affected by it. The one acts upon the other and every abiding change in the life of man is the result of these mutual reactions.

No movement in the world directs its attention upon both these aspects of human life and has full measures for their improvement, save the teachings of Bahá'u'lláh. And this is its distinctive feature. If we desire therefore the good of the world we should strive to spread those teachings and also practice them in our own life. Through them will the human heart be changed, and also our social environment provides the atmosphere in which we can grow spiritually and reflect in full the light of God shining through the revelation of Bahá'u'lláh. (qtd. in *Compilation* 84)[30]

---

30   In certain instances, some Bahá'ís may feel obstructed from taking action by the majority view of other Bahá'ís. It is then hoped that through the study of particular courses, the attitudes of the majority might change. It is not practical to expect, however, that transformation of the community can occur in this way. And significant progress cannot be achieved if the actions of those who are most capable to take on the challenges of addressing community building or racial prejudice are held back by those who are, perhaps, least prepared to take on this work. The current series of Plans is organized in such a way to enable all individuals to take initial constructive action within their own core activities and neighborhoods, and to learn how to improve their efforts over time. And as this lived experience to promote the oneness of humanity becomes richer and deeper, more and more will be attracted to take their place in the process of translating Bahá'u'lláh teachings about oneness into reality and action. Those who become enamored with the Faith in such settings can be taught the Faith and deepened in their understanding before being introduced to the wider community, where some concerns might exist. As Shoghi Effendi explains the process of reaching new souls: "Let him refrain, at the outset, from insisting on such laws and observances as might impose too severe a strain on the seeker's newly awakened faith, and endeavor to nurse him, patiently, tactfully, and yet determinedly, into full maturity, and aid him to proclaim his unqualified acceptance of whatever has been ordained by Bahá'u'lláh. Let him, as soon as that stage has been attained, introduce him to the body of his fellow-believers, and seek, through constant fellowship and active participation in the local activities of his community, to enable him to contribute his share to the enrichment of its life, the furtherance of its tasks, the consolidations of its interests, and the coordination of its activities with those of its sister communities. Let him not be content until he has infused into his spiritual child so deep a longing as to impel him to arise independently, in his turn, and devote his energies to the quickening of other souls, and the upholding of the laws and principles laid down by his newly adopted Faith" (*Advent* 51–52).

Such is the actualization of the process described above, in which spiritualized human beings see the essence of each person as the divine endowment within and develop the God-given potentialities inherent in their souls as they strive to live according to the teachings of Bahá'u'lláh. Together such illumined souls learn to traverse a defective, racialized social reality and transform it, beginning within the social spaces which they create and in which they participate, eliminating these racialized features and creating a social reality of oneness expressed as unity in diversity.

Consider how activities unfold in a cluster and how they contribute to a new set of relationships among people that reflect the oneness of humanity.

Central to the progress of the Plan is the training institute, whose purpose is to build the capabilities of individuals to translate Bahá'u'lláh's teachings into action to advance the work of community building, social action, and involvement in the discourses of society. Beginning with Book 1, participants learn how to understand the sacred writings, the importance of prayer, and the purpose of life. As a result, they begin to practice daily prayer and reading of the writings, along with taking daily account for personal behavior—the basic spiritual disciplines that serve as the foundation of personal transformation. They then begin to work with others engaged in a similar process of collective change by initiating action with a devotional gathering—an initial act of service. Each of the books of the institute builds new capabilities for additional acts of service that propel the transformation of individuals and communities.

The institute process also raises a program for the education of young people. Cohorts of children enter children's classes that shape their spiritual and social development. This is followed by their junior youth groups that endow them with the power of expression, provide initial experience in undertaking acts of service for the common good, and quicken their desire to immerse themselves in the knowledge systems of science and religion so they can better fulfill their twofold moral purpose. As youth, they begin the sequence of courses of the institute to build their capabilities to take their place in the program of growth along with a growing number of others.

As more and more capable participants enter the arena of action, gradually, a pattern of community life emerges composed of a variety of social spaces that are created and broadened through the inclusion of more and more people. These social spaces include core activities and other gatherings, efforts within neighborhoods and across the cluster, projects for social action and opportunities for engaging others in discourses of various kinds. This pattern of community life also includes family life, all Bahá'í gatherings, and, essentially, every social space in which Bahá'ís participate. The aim of a program of growth is not merely to reach out to others to participate in activities, but ultimately, to endow populations with ownership and empower them to become the protagonists of the process of personal and social transformation, and thus to release the society-building power of Bahá'u'lláh's Revelation in ever greater measures.

Core activities and other dimensions of the community building process can be understood as liminal spaces—social spaces of transition—that can transcend the understanding and practices of the old world order, but that do not yet reflect the characteristics of the new world order that is yet to be fully realized. In such transitional spaces, new ways of thinking, new ways of interacting, new ways of living not shackled by the cultural limitations of societies structured along lines of contention and otherness can begin to emerge. These spaces are thus a starting point for the transformation, discussed above, that all peoples must undergo in order to play their part in the building of a new global civilization. In them, participants can begin the process of weighing their culture in light of Bahá'u'lláh's teachings to determine which gifts it has to offer and which of its limitations must be purged. For the people of India, transformation may involve coming to terms with the negative ramifications of the caste system. For the people of the Democratic Republic of the Congo, it may require addressing conflicts that emerge from ethnicity. And in the United States, it demands dealing with the evil tendency of racial prejudice. Such transitional spaces can embrace all in the oneness of humanity, freed of any burden of otherness, while at the same time, ensuring that those gathered within a particular space do not fail to address any racially prejudicial practices, or their consequences, that intrude upon them. In this manner, Bahá'í community building activities offer an escape from the catch-22 that prevents progress towards a non-racialized social order.

The release in greater measure of the society-building power of the Bahá'í Faith is dependent upon the creation, in every cluster, of a pattern of life illumined by Bahá'u'lláh's Revelation. To bring this new pattern of life into being, and to foster its development and complexity over time to create a new world order, requires new capabilities of individuals, communities, and institutions. If a certain cluster does not manifest this society building power, it is because the necessary capabilities of the three protagonists have not been sufficiently cultivated. Where it is lacking, a particular capability can be identified as a learning objective. It is the purpose of the institute to cultivate such capabilities, which are refined in action in the work of community building. The institute fosters a basic set of capabilities for creating an ever-expanding community building process in light of Bahá'u'lláh's teaching, and as learning about the release of the society building power of the Faith to address the challenge of racial prejudice advances, additional capabilities to support this process can be better understood and consciously developed. As all these necessary capabilities are cultivated through experience and learning over time, the people of a cluster will increasingly manifest the necessary change.[31]

The National Spiritual Assembly of the United States has reported on the current nature of the efforts underway in scores of programs of growth across the country, in hundreds of initiatives for social action addressing issues pertaining to race, and in the contributions of thousands of individual believers to discourses in civil society, in their professions, and in their local communities.[32] It is striving to establish a national process to facilitate learning to advance these efforts. The series of Plans now unfolding will continually multiply and expand the social spaces in which Bahá'ís participate, and where they can, in keeping with the vision of the Guardian, bring into practice the Bahá'í teachings on the

---

31   Examples of the profound transformative effect on social reality made possible by the community building process can be found in the 2013 video, *Frontiers of Learning*, in relation to alleviating problems associated with the caste system and with opportunities for women in India.

32   For more details, see *A Spiritual Path to Unity and Social Justice: The Bahá'í Faith in America.*

elimination of prejudice, whether directly or indirectly. Beyond the multiplication of such a broad range of efforts, the elimination of racial prejudice in American society will require a sound learning process that can weigh the wide range of initiatives across many clusters and neighborhoods, so that those that prove to be effective may be further refined and systematically shared and applied in more and more localities.

Discussions about race or issues associated with race can be very challenging and sensitive, involving difficult truths and a host of emotions. An inability to maintain a constructive approach and willingness to learn can create the potential for extremes of conflict or avoidance that thwart progress. But the spaces being created serve as active workshops for learning and change. In such settings, mistakes will sometimes be made, and on occasion problems will arise. Yet, it is precisely in such settings that the participants, seeing themselves as one and dedicated to a common purpose, can respond with love and forbearance to resolve any issues that emerge and continue their progress to achieve ever-higher levels of understanding and action over time.

Learning and the Ultimate Elimination of Racial Prejudice

THE PROCESS OF LEARNING DESCRIBED BY THE UNIVERSAL HOUSE of Justice involving study, consultation, action and reflection is, of course, a fundamental aspect of the evolving framework for action encompassing the work of the Nine Year Plan, and it is equally central to the framework as it is applied toward the elimination of racial prejudice. Indeed, this process is at the heart of progress in every area of endeavor in the Bahá'í world. When efforts are approached in a mode of learning, they generally begin simply and grow in complexity over time, as insights emerge and methods that prove to be effective are refined and disseminated. The reading of reality in a social space becomes increasingly accurate and comprehensive, and understanding of relevant portions of Bahá'u'lláh's teachings and the guidance provided by the House of Justice is enhanced and deepened. As the Riḍván 2010 message of the House of Justice to the Bahá'ís of the world explains:

understanding the implications of the Revelation, both in terms of individual growth and social progress, increases manifold when study and service are joined and carried out concurrently. There, in the field of service, knowledge is tested, questions arise out of practice, and new levels of understanding are achieved.

Engagement in a process of learning for social change requires an historical perspective—a sense of movement along a path over time. Hence the questions set out in describing the nature of a framework for action earlier in this paper: Where were we? Where are we now? How did we get from where we were to where we are now? Where are we going? How can we get there?

These are the fundamental questions that the Bahá'í community continually reflects upon to understand the developmental path that it is traversing and learn how to navigate its course along that path into the future. If we have a sense of where we are trying to go, we can analyze our efforts to determine whether we are getting closer to that intended destination or not. If certain efforts prove to be effective, they can be spread to other areas and multiplied. If problems or obstacles arise in our path, objectives for learning can be specified to concentrate efforts on how to overcome them. Over time, practical experience is measured against the vision of the way forward to determine if there is progress, or whether action needs to be revised, or the vision refocused. Principles established by 'Abdu'l-Bahá and Shoghi Effendi, as well as the timely counsels provided by the Universal House of Justice, illuminate the ongoing learning process that guides the progress of efforts aimed at the elimination of racial prejudice. A letter written on behalf of the House of Justice to an individual outlines the importance of reflection on this movement and evolution as progress is made into the future:

> As you continue your noteworthy efforts to advance along the path laid out in that letter, you should keep in mind the fundamental difference between your work in the past to promote race unity and your efforts today. Whereas before you were implementing a centralized program initiated at the national level that involved friends across the country in

what they easily understood to be a single endeavor, today, you are promoting a unity in diversity of actions, emerging largely from the grassroots, in pursuit of this aim. Many of the perceptions you describe can be understood in light of the difficulty in conveying how these seemingly unconnected elements all contribute to a common enterprise. Yet only through such a decentralized approach that is coherent with the framework for action of the Plan can the contribution of the American Bahá'í community to fundamental, sustained, spiritual and social transformation gradually grow in scale and effectiveness—through action and reflection over time—until it has a profound effect on the wider society. As the House of Justice explained in a letter written on its behalf to the National Assembly, "it is not predominantly by means of offering special courses and programs on race within the Bahá'í community that racial issues will be overcome. Instead, it is through collective action in the various social spaces in which the friends are wholeheartedly engaged to translate the Teachings into action that they will, through mistakes and difficulties, with love and forbearance, learn to resolve challenges pertaining to race, both within their communities and in the society at large." (24 March 2019)

Consultation enables people with differing viewpoints to find agreement in the search for solutions; consensus is then tested in action to determine if a certain approach proves to be effective. In the discourse of the wider society, it is not uncommon for personal animosity to arise between those who hold competing perspectives or recommend alternative solutions. In consultation, however, love and mutual respect are maintained even in the face of strong initial disagreements. As diverse ideas are shared, individuals detach themselves from their personal opinions, listen to others, and accept new insights, until a consensus emerges—whether held unanimously or by a majority. In this way, individuals harmonize their views, reach a collective decision, and then implement it together in unity to determine whether it is effective or, if necessary, to determine how to revise action over time. Through the institute process and the work of community building, the capabilities for consultation and learning are cultivated and social spaces for action and reflection are established. Gradually, these capabilities proliferate, and the spaces expand and multiply, to include more and more participants in unified thought and action, whether Bahá'ís or others.

As this unity in diversity of activities emerges in communities and neighborhoods across the country, it will receive direction and focus from the learning process that takes place at the regional and national level. Through its race unity desk and other entities, the National Assembly can ensure the facilitation of a national process of learning about the elimination of racial prejudice, as one aspect of the work of the Bahá'í community that is coherent with all other endeavors. Such entities can provide a variety of means—including compilations, case studies, seminars, reflection gatherings, analysis of promising approaches, and proposals for future action—to assist the National Assembly and Counsellors to support and guide the efforts of the community. In this way, experiences of proven effectiveness can be identified and widely shared so that the community's endeavors can be continually refined and strengthened until they can achieve a pronounced effect on the elimination of racial prejudice in the wider society.

When the Four Year Plan began in 1996, it was impossible to conceive of the exact nature of the approaches the worldwide community would adopt by 2021 to advance the process of growth and community building. Step by step, learning shaped progress, ultimately giving rise to systematic efforts and methods of proven effectiveness for community building, social action and involvement in the discourses of society that have extended to millions of people in thousands of clusters across the planet.

So too, it is not currently possible to see exactly how the path toward the elimination of racial prejudice will unfold through the series of Plans up to 2046, much less until the point where the full implications of the hopes of 'Abdu'l-Bahá and Shoghi Effendi are realized. Yet step by step, learning will shape progress for the elimination of racial prejudice; this is an inseparable part of the mission of the American Bahá'í community in the years ahead. As Shoghi Effendi emphatically states, the friends must be

> ever mindful that every intensification of effort on their part
> will better equip them for the time when they will be called

upon to eradicate in their turn such evil tendencies from the lives and the hearts of the entire body of their fellow-citizens. Nor must they overlook the fact that the World Order, whose basis they, as the advance-guard of the future Bahá'í generations of their countrymen, are now laboring to establish, can never be reared unless and until the generality of the people to which they belong has been already purged from the divers ills, whether social or political, that now so severely afflict it. (*Advent* 20–21)

Some Thoughts on the Individual who Contributes to the Elimination of Racial Prejudice

A REFLECTION ON THE ELIMINATION OF RACIAL PREJUDICE WOULD not be complete without consideration of the capabilities required of the individual who arises as a protagonist to achieve Bahá'u'lláh's aim for the ultimate elimination of racial prejudice in the United States. Ultimately the change in society depends upon the spiritual transformation of individuals and the expression of spiritual principles and qualities.

An initial problem presents itself as we try to find a useful term to identify such an individual. "Promoter of the oneness of humanity" seems to fail to grasp the racial dimension of the challenge at all. "Promoter of racial justice" may imply an intention to organize relationships in society to uphold some essential of race—a set of just relations among perpetually distinct peoples. Even the modest concept of "promoter of racial harmony" seems insufficient, suggesting attention to only an early stage on the long path of learning that leads to the building of a society entirely free of the effects of racial prejudice. And so, language again presents a trap that confines understanding and action. Nevertheless, by any descriptor, it is useful to consider at least some of the essential capabilities of such a protagonist from a Bahá'í perspective, which may not perfectly overlap with the characteristics often associated with those committed to combatting racism in contemporary society.

The observations presented above show how the perspective on the challenge of racial prejudice found in Bahá'u'lláh's teachings frees Bahá'ís from becoming ensnared in the intractable disputes associated with the catch-22 of colorblindness and essentialism. In a contest of values, identity, methods, and beliefs, there is no way to avoid conflict and an endless morphing of the problem from one form to another. Bahá'ís find a way beyond the apparent dichotomy through a harmonious embrace of both oneness and diversity. In the light of Bahá'u'lláh's teachings, the debates swirling in contemporary society about whether there is a problem, who is responsible, and what the goal ought to be, are settled matters for Bahá'ís.

Every Bahá'í, within the limitations of personal capacity, embraces and promulgates the principle of the oneness of humanity—the consummate repudiation of any notion of racial superiority. At the same time, because the existing social order is shaped by deep historical and contemporary understanding and actions that have given rise to intractable individual and institutionalized forms of racial prejudice, no Bahá'í can claim to be completely free of its influence—although perhaps each is affected in different ways. And thus, every Bahá'í, of whatever background, has a responsibility to contribute to the resolution of the challenge presented by racial prejudice, both in their own lives and in the life of society. As Shoghi Effendi explains, every Bahá'í "must participate in, and lend their assistance, each according to his or her capacity, experience, and opportunities, to the common task of fulfilling the instructions, realizing the hopes, and following the example, of 'Abdu'l-Bahá." And he continues, as alluded to above: "neither race has the right, or can conscientiously claim, to be regarded as absolved from such an obligation, as having realized such hopes, or having faithfully followed such an example" (*Advent* 33)

With the embrace of the oneness of humanity, attention can be directed to the nature of the relationships necessary to achieve a social order that celebrates diversity but is free of the evil tendency of racial prejudice. The individual who works toward such an objective becomes a protagonist not in the sense of contending with others, but in the sense of reaching out and building a network of sound relationships through constructive engagement with others. The instrument of change is not coercion, but moral persuasion and cooperation through both example and speech. Within specific social spaces, a pattern of life can be raised—ever-expanding in reach and depth—that manifests racial unity in place of prejudice and conflict. The catalyst for change, as the House of Justice explained, is love:

> Ultimately, the power to transform the world is effected by love, love originating from the relationship with the divine, love ablaze among members of a community, love extended without restriction to every human being. This divine love, ignited by the Word of God, is disseminated by enkindled souls through intimate conversations that create new susceptibilities in human hearts, open minds to moral persuasion, and loosen the hold of biased norms and social systems so that they can gradually take on a new form in keeping with the requirements of humanity's age of maturity. You are channels for this divine love; let it flow through you to all who cross your path. Infuse it into every neighborhood and social space in which you move to build capacity to canalize the society-building power of Bahá'u'lláh's Revelation. There can be no rest until the destined outcome is achieved. (*Messages 2001–2022* ¶ 374.5)

In this effort, the House of Justice adds, 'Abdu'l-Bahá is not only each protagonist's "solace and support" but also the example and guide: "wise in His approach, penetrating in utterance, indiscriminating in fellowship, unfailing in sympathy for the downtrodden, courageous in conduct, persevering in action, imperturbable in the face of tests, unwavering in His keen sense of justice" (*Messages 2001–2022* ¶ 374.6).

The Bahá'í teachings are replete with guidance about how to comport oneself to create constructive change. All that guidance can be applied by the individual who arises to promote the change required to eliminate racial prejudice in America. This includes Bahá'u'lláh's prohibitions on backbiting, on conflict and contention, and judging and criticizing the personal faults of others. Speech, the Bahá'í teachings make evident, must meet certain conditions to achieve constructive influence. Lasting change emerges from building new ways of being and doing that reshape human relationships to reflect oneness and unity. An individual who arises to promote justice will, inevitably, endure injustice.

The abundant advice found in the Bahá'í writings about how to teach the Faith, although too extensive to repeat here, offers useful insights into on how to draw others into the constructive process of building new relationships that overcome the manifestations of racial prejudice. One engages in kindly persuasion, not instruction and insisting on what is right. Loving bonds are formed to remove veils, since people tend to respond to those who are close to them. One serves as leaven to influence change rather than exercising force and coercion. The best teacher adapts methods to meet the needs of the seeker. Approaches may be direct or indirect. One must sometimes mark time, and sometimes act swiftly. Effective social change begins simply and through experience grows in complexity over time.

As a program of growth becomes more complex and reaches ever greater numbers, individuals have a good deal of latitude to determine how to direct their energies. This takes place in settings where participants are racially diverse, and in others where they are not. Challenges arising from racial prejudice in a specific social setting may be addressed directly or indirectly, depending on circumstances.

For example, a particular personal initiative may directly address problems associated with race. This can take a form associated with community building with other like-minded individuals, such as a regular devotional meeting that includes discussions associated with race, or an initiative for social action pertaining to challenges within a particular neighborhood. It may also take the form of involvement in a discourse within the wider society, in a setting such as one's workplace or school, or the study of certain books or course material.

It is also possible and perhaps even more likely that a personal initiative would address the challenge of racial prejudice from an indirect perspective, seeking, without explicitly mentioning race, to build new relationships that reflect the oneness of humanity, or to redress certain social ills resulting from prejudice. This could include a wide range of community building activities, which begin with a focus on topics that do not specifically address race.

It might include projects for social action such as supporting the academic efforts of those in a junior youth group whose schooling has been disadvantaged by social inequalities. The choice of personal initiatives may well vary in neighborhoods that are diverse, as opposed to those that are homogenous. Without reifying racial categories, the many impacts and injustices of a racialized social order can be addressed.

From a Bahá'í perspective, the end of racial prejudice will come largely from building the oneness of humanity—an organic change in the structure of society, the reconstruction of the world—rather than from directly fighting racism. This does not mean that the activities a person undertakes cannot directly address the problem of racial prejudice in different ways. It does mean, however, that those who choose to engage in such activities cannot presume that others who do not do so are therefore uninvolved in the vital work of eliminating the problem.

The prerogative of individuals does not extend to insisting upon the correctness of one's personal views and imposing them on others within the available social spaces, or to insisting that communities or institutions must adopt one's personal views and plans of action for the entire community. In the areas of collective endeavor, it is the process of consultation and the decisions of relevant institutions that determine how the community will proceed. Naturally, an individual that participates in the collective process can make recommendations for action. But the unity of the community is preserved by adherence to Bahá'í principles. At the same time, the importance of collective endeavor does not mean that some who do not understand the challenges associated with racial prejudice should obstruct the efforts of others to find solutions.

A letter written on behalf of the Guardian to an individual captures the way in which constructive social change can be effected by a dedicated soul.

You must not make the great mistake of judging our Faith by one community which obviously needs to study and obey the Bahá'í teachings. Human frailties and peculiarities can be a great test. But the only way, or perhaps I should say the first and best way, to remedy such situations, is to oneself do what is right. One soul can be the cause of the spiritual illumination of a continent. Now that you have seen, and remedied, a great fault in your own life, now that you see more clearly what is lacking in your own community, there is nothing to prevent you from arising and showing such an example, such a love and spirit of service, as to enkindle the heart of your fellow Bahá'ís.

He urges you to study deeply the teachings, teach others, study with those Bahá'ís who are anxious to do so, the deeper teachings of our Faith, and through example, effort and prayer, bring about a change. (in *Compilation* 230)

Thus, for Bahá'ís, the attempt to transform social reality is starkly different from common approaches found in the wider society—to find fault, take sides and fight, and condemn those whose ideas and practices are not in conformity with ones' own. No matter how convinced an individual may be of his or her personal understanding and approach, lasting change cannot be achieved by sacrificing the relevant spiritual principles.

Conclusion

The vision of a coherent, systematic, and sustainable approach to eliminate racial prejudice in the United States, which is conducted within the context of an evolving framework for action, is fundamental to the mission of the American Bahá'í community.

In *The Advent of Divine Justice*, where Shoghi Effendi calls for a response by the Bahá'ís to the three evil tendencies afflicting the people of the American nation, he envisions that the mission of the community would extend beyond its global responsibilities as chief executors of the Divine Plan. He writes:

And who knows but that when this colossal task has been accomplished a greater, a still more superb mission, incomparable in its splendor, and foreordained for them by Bahá'u'lláh, may not be thrust upon them? The glories of such a mission are of such dazzling splendor, the circumstances attending it so remote, and the contemporary events with the culmination of which it is so closely knit in such a state of flux, that it would be premature to attempt, at the present time, any accurate delineation of its features. Suffice it to say that out of the turmoil and tribulations of these "latter years" opportunities undreamt of will be born, and circumstances unpredictable created, that will enable, nay impel, the victorious prosecutors of 'Abdu'l-Bahá's Plan, to add, through the part they will play in the unrolling of the New World Order, fresh laurels to the crown of their servitude to the threshold of Bahá'u'lláh. (13)

Shoghi Effendi ties this mission not only to the destiny of the American nation envisioned by 'Abdu'l-Bahá, but also to the eventual emergence of the World Order of Bahá'u'lláh. Thus, the contribution the Bahá'í community must make to the elimination of racial prejudice in America is vital and pressing as it strives to release, in various ways and in ever increasing measures, the society-building power of the Faith. The Guardian promised that the time would come when the community would be called to such a responsibility, and the House of Justice has made it emphatically clear that "That time has now come" (28 November 2024). The community will fulfill its responsibility by the movement of its clusters "to the farthest frontiers of learning."[33]

For many years, race unity has been a constructive starting point for addressing the challenges of race in society. But the elimination of racialization itself is the ultimate objective of the Bahá'í teachings—that differences of race should be annulled as Bahá'u'lláh explained. It may be difficult to imagine how the current conception of race promulgated in the United States over four centuries will disappear and be replaced by a conception of unity in diversity that can scarcely be imagined at this time.[34]

33   The Universal House of Justice, 26 March 2016, *Messages of the Universal House of Justice, 2001-2022*, para. 256.3.

34   To imagine how social transformation can be practically realized, see for example, *The Upswing: How America Came Together a Century Ago and How We Can Do It Again*, by Robert Putnam. It was the beginning of this change that 'Abdu'l-Bahá encountered and reinforced during His visit to America. Through the application of Bahá'u'lláh's teachings it is possible to envision a social transformation that does not deteriorate, and that can eventually give rise to the emergence of the lesser peace. After a deep analysis of

What is certain, however, is that if we can learn over time within an evolving framework for action, our understanding and capacity for action will consistently deepen, Plan by Plan. And by the culmination of the current series of Plans, it will be possible to witness a profound transformation in our community and in society as a whole.

---

the impact of systemic racism in the book *Metaracism*, author Tricia Rose proposes a path to finding a solution in a cultural paradigm shift and the ability to find specific leverage points for practical change. She writes: "In the sharing and cocreating of communities where we expand, enrich, and rehabilitate one another, we forge the bonds and interconnections of systemic justice." The work of the Bahá'í world is to build such communities based on the unprecedented cultural paradigm shift characterized by Bahá'u'lláh's principle of the oneness of humanity; within these communities, individuals, communities, and institutions can increasingly learn to identify the impact of racism in its various forms and to take practical action to transform the social reality within neighborhoods and up to the national level.

Selected Passages Pertaining to the Elimination of Racial Prejudice

FROM THE WRITINGS OF BAHÁ'U'LLÁH

— *1* —

The All-Knowing Physician hath His finger on the pulse of mankind. He perceiveth the disease, and prescribeth, in His unerring wisdom, the remedy. Every age hath its own problem, and every soul its particular aspiration. The remedy the world needeth in its present-day afflictions can never be the same as that which a subsequent age may require. Be anxiously concerned with the needs of the age ye live in, and center your deliberations on its exigencies and requirements.

We can well perceive how the whole human race is encompassed with great, with incalculable afflictions. We see it languishing on its bed of sickness, sore-tried and disillusioned. They that are intoxicated by self-conceit have interposed themselves between it and the Divine and infallible Physician. Witness how they have entangled all men, themselves included, in the mesh of their devices. They can neither discover the cause of the disease, nor have they any knowledge of the remedy. They have conceived the straight to be crooked, and have imagined their friend an enemy.

Gleanings from the Writings of Bahá'u'lláh, p. 212

— *2* —

The Great Being saith: O ye children of men! The fundamental purpose animating the Faith of God and His Religion is to safeguard the interests and promote the unity of the human race, and to foster the spirit of love and fellowship amongst men. Suffer it not to become a source of dissension and discord, of hate and enmity. This is the straight Path, the fixed and immovable foundation. Whatsoever is raised on this foundation, the changes and chances of the world can never impair its strength, nor will the revolution of countless centuries undermine its structure. Our hope is that the world's religious leaders and the rulers thereof will unitedly arise for the reformation of this age and the rehabilitation of its fortunes. Let them, after meditating on its needs, take counsel together and, through anxious and full deliberation, administer to a diseased and sorely-afflicted world the remedy it requireth. . . . Please God, the peoples of the world may be led, as the result of the high endeavors exerted by their rulers and the wise and learned amongst men, to recognize their best interests. How long will humanity persist in its waywardness? How long will injustice continue? How long is chaos and confusion to reign amongst men? How long will discord agitate the face of society? . . . The winds of despair are, alas, blowing from every direction, and the strife that divideth and afflicteth the human race is daily increasing. The signs of impending convulsions and chaos can now be discerned, inasmuch as the prevailing order appeareth to be lamentably defective. I beseech God, exalted be His glory, that He may graciously awaken the peoples of the earth, may grant that the end of their conduct may be profitable unto them, and aid them to accomplish that which beseemeth their station.

Gleanings from the Writings of Bahá'u'lláh, pp. 215-16

— 3 —

He Who is your Lord, the All-Merciful, cherisheth in His heart the desire of beholding the entire human race as one soul and one body. Haste ye to win your share of God's good grace and mercy in this Day that eclipseth all other created Days. How great the felicity that awaiteth the man that forsaketh all he hath in a desire to obtain the things of God! Such a man, We testify, is among God's blessed ones.

Gleanings from the Writings of Bahá'u'lláh, p. 213

— *4* —

O contending peoples and kindreds of the earth! Set your faces towards unity, and let the radiance of its light shine upon you. Gather ye together, and for the sake of God resolve to root out whatever is the source of contention amongst you. Then will the effulgence of the world's great Luminary envelop the whole earth, and its inhabitants become the citizens of one city, and the occupants of one and the same throne. This wronged One hath, ever since the early days of His life, cherished none other desire but this, and will continue to entertain no wish except this wish. There can be no doubt whatever that the peoples of the world, of whatever race or religion, derive their inspiration from one heavenly Source, and are the subjects of one God. . . . Arise and, armed with the power of faith, shatter to pieces the gods of your vain imaginings, the sowers of dissension amongst you. Cleave unto that which draweth you together and uniteth you.

Gleanings from the Writings of Bahá'u'lláh, pp. 216-17

— *5* —

O CHILDREN OF MEN! Know ye not why We created you all from the same dust? That no one should exalt himself over the other. Ponder at all times in your hearts how ye were created. Since We have created you all from one same substance it is incumbent on you to be even as one soul, to walk with the same feet, eat with the same mouth and dwell in the same land, that from your inmost being, by your deeds and actions, the signs of oneness and the essence of detachment may be made manifest. Such is My counsel to you, O concourse of light! Heed ye this counsel that ye may obtain the fruit of holiness from the tree of wondrous glory.

The Hidden Words, Arabic #68

— *6* —

We desire but the good of the world and the happiness of the nations; yet they deem Us a stirrer up of strife and sedition worthy of bondage and banishment. . . . That all nations should become one in faith and all men as brothers; that the bonds of affection and unity between the sons of men should be strengthened; that diversity of religion should cease, and differences of race be annulled—what harm is there in this? . . . Yet so it shall be; these fruitless strifes, these ruinous wars shall pass away, and the 'Most Great Peace' shall come.

The Proclamation of Bahá'u'lláh, p. viii

— 7 —

O ye discerning ones! Verily, the words which have descended from the heaven of the Will of God are the source of unity and harmony for the world. Close your eyes to racial differences, and welcome all with the light of oneness.

The Advent of Divine Justice, p. 37

— 8 —

It is incumbent upon every man of insight and understanding to strive to translate that which hath been written into reality and action. . . . That one indeed is a man who, today, dedicateth himself to the service of the entire human race. The Great Being saith: Blessed and happy is he that ariseth to promote the best interests of the peoples and kindreds of the earth. In another passage He hath proclaimed: It is not for him to pride himself who loveth his own country, but rather for him who loveth the whole world. The earth is but one country, and mankind its citizens.

Gleanings from the Writings of Bahá'u'lláh, p. 249

FROM THE TALKS AND WRITINGS OF 'ABDU'L-BAHÁ

— 9 —

Praise be to God, throughout succeeding centuries and ages the call of civilization hath been raised, the world of humanity hath been advancing and progressing day by day, various countries have been developing by leaps and bounds, and material improvements have increased, until the world of existence obtained universal capacity to receive the spiritual teachings and to hearken to the Divine Call. The suckling babe passeth through various physical stages, growing and developing at every stage, until its body reacheth the age of maturity. Having arrived at this stage it acquireth the capacity to manifest spiritual and intellectual perfections. The lights of comprehension, intelligence and knowledge become perceptible in it and the powers of its soul unfold. Similarly, in the contingent world, the human species hath undergone progressive physical changes and, by a slow process, hath scaled the ladder of civilization, realizing in itself the wonders, excellencies and gifts of humanity in their most glorious form, until it gained the capacity to express the splendours of spiritual perfections and divine ideals and became capable of hearkening to the call of God. Then at last the call of the Kingdom was raised, the spiritual virtues and perfections were revealed, the Sun of Reality dawned, and the teachings of the Most Great Peace, of the oneness of the world of humanity and of the universality of men, were promoted. We hope that the effulgence of these rays shall become more and more intense, and the ideal virtues more resplendent, so that the goal of this universal human process will be attained and the love of God will appear in the utmost grace and beauty and bedazzle all hearts.

O ye beloved of God! Know ye, verily, that the happiness of mankind lieth in the unity and the harmony of the human race, and that spiritual and material developments are conditioned upon love and amity among all men. . . .

Similarly, consider how the cause of the welfare, happiness, joy and comfort of humankind are amity and union, whereas dissension and discord are most conducive to hardship, humiliation, agitation and failure.

But a thousand times alas, that man is negligent and unaware of these facts, and daily doth he strut abroad with the characteristics of a wild beast. Lo! At one moment he turneth into a ferocious tiger; at the next he becometh a creeping, venomous viper! But the sublime achievements of man reside in those qualities and attributes that exclusively pertain to the angels of the Supreme Concourse. Therefore, when praiseworthy qualities and high morals emanate from man, he becometh a heavenly being, an angel of the Kingdom, a divine reality and a celestial effulgence. On the other hand, when he engageth in warfare, quarrelling and bloodshed, he becometh viler than the most fierce of savage creatures, for if a bloodthirsty wolf devoureth a lamb in a single night, man slaughtereth a hundred thousand in the field of battle, strewing the ground with their corpses and kneading the earth with their blood.

In short, man is endowed with two natures: one tendeth towards moral sublimity and intellectual perfection, while the other turneth to bestial degradation and carnal imperfections. If ye travel the countries of the globe ye shall observe on one side the remains of ruin and destruction, while on the other ye shall see the signs of civilization and development. Such desolation and ruin are the result of war, strife and quarrelling, while all development and progress are fruits of the lights of virtue, co-operation and concord. . . .

A critic may object, saying that peoples, races, tribes and communities of the world are of different and varied customs, habits, tastes, character, inclinations and ideas, that opinions and thoughts are contrary to one another, and how, therefore, is it possible for real unity to be revealed and perfect accord among human souls to exist?

In answer we say that differences are of two kinds. One is the cause of annihilation and is like the antipathy existing among warring nations and conflicting tribes who seek each other's destruction, uprooting one another's families, depriving one another of rest and comfort and unleashing carnage. The other kind which is a token of diversity is the essence of perfection and the cause of the appearance of the bestowals of the Most Glorious Lord.

Consider the flowers of a garden: though differing in kind, colour, form and shape, yet, inasmuch as they are refreshed by the waters of one spring, revived by the breath of one wind, invigorated by the rays of one sun, this diversity increaseth their charm, and addeth unto their beauty. Thus when that unifying force, the penetrating influence of the Word of God, taketh effect, the difference of customs, manners, habits, ideas, opinions and dispositions embellisheth the world of humanity. This diversity, this difference is like the naturally created dissimilarity and variety of the limbs and organs of the human body, for each one contributeth to the beauty, efficiency and perfection of the whole.

When these different limbs and organs come under the influence of man's sovereign soul, and the soul's power pervadeth the limbs and members, veins and arteries of the body, then difference reinforceth harmony, diversity strengtheneth love, and multiplicity is the greatest factor for co-ordination.

How unpleasing to the eye if all the flowers and plants, the leaves and blossoms, the fruits, the branches and the trees of that garden were all of the same shape and colour! Diversity of hues, form and shape, enricheth and adorneth the garden, and heighteneth the effect thereof. In like manner, when divers shades of thought, temperament and character, are brought together under the power and influence of one central agency, the beauty and glory of human perfection will be revealed and made manifest. Naught but the celestial potency of the Word of God, which ruleth and transcendeth the realities of all things, is capable of harmonizing the divergent thoughts, sentiments, ideas, and convictions of the children of men. Verily, it is the penetrating power in all things, the mover of souls and the binder and regulator in the world of humanity.

Praise be to God, today the splendour of the Word of God hath illumined every horizon, and from all sects, races, tribes, nations, and communities souls have come together in the light of the Word, assembled, united and agreed in perfect harmony. Oh! What a great number of meetings are held adorned with souls from various races and diverse sects! Anyone attending these will be struck with amazement, and might suppose that these souls are all of one land, one nationality, one community, one thought, one belief and one opinion; whereas, in fact, one is an American, the other an African, one cometh from Asia and another from Europe, one is a native of India, another is from Turkestan, one is an Arab, another a Tajik, another a Persian and yet another a Greek. Notwithstanding such diversity they associate in perfect harmony and unity, love and freedom; they have one voice, one thought and one purpose. Verily, this is from the penetrative power of the Word of God! If all the forces of the universe were to combine they would not be able thus to gather a single assemblage so imbued with the sentiments of love, affection, attraction and enkindlement as to unite the members of different races and to raise up from the heart of the world a voice that shall dispel war and strife, uproot dissension and disputation, usher in the era of universal peace and establish unity and concord amongst men.

Can any power withstand the penetrative influence of the Word of God? Nay, by God! The proof is clear and the evidence is complete! If anyone looketh with the eyes of justice he shall be struck with wonder and amazement and will testify that all the peoples, sects and races of the world should be glad, content and grateful for the teachings and admonitions of Bahá'u'lláh. For these divine injunctions tame every ferocious beast, transform the creeping insect into a soaring bird, cause human souls to become angels of the Kingdom, and make the human world a focus for the qualities of mercy.

Selections from the Writings of 'Abdu'l-Bahá, pp. 285-93

— 10 —

The teachings specialized in Bahá'u'lláh are addressed to humanity. He says, "Ye are all the leaves of one tree." He does not say, "Ye are the leaves of two trees: one divine, the other satanic." He has declared that each individual member of the human family is a leaf or branch upon the Adamic tree; that all are sheltered beneath the protecting mercy and providence of God; that all are the children of God, fruit upon the one tree of His love. God is equally compassionate and kind to all the leaves, branches and fruit of this tree. Therefore, there is no satanic tree whatever—Satan being a product of human minds and of instinctive human tendencies toward error. God alone is Creator, and all are creatures of His might. Therefore, we must love mankind as His creatures, realizing that all are growing upon the tree of His mercy, servants of His omnipotent will and manifestations of His good pleasure.

The Promulgation of Universal Peace, pp. 230-31

— 11 —

And among the teachings of Bahá'u'lláh is, that religious, racial, political, economic and patriotic prejudices destroy the edifice of humanity. As long as these prejudices prevail, the world of humanity will not have rest. For a period of 6,000 years history informs us about the world of humanity. During these 6,000 years the world of humanity has not been free from, war, strife, murder and bloodthirstiness. In every period war has been waged in one country or another and that war was due to either religious prejudice, racial prejudice, political prejudice or patriotic prejudice. It has therefore been ascertained and proved that all prejudices are destructive of the human edifice. As long as these prejudices persist, the struggle for existence must remain dominant, and bloodthirstiness and rapacity continue. Therefore, even as was the case in the past, the world of humanity cannot be saved from the darkness of nature and cannot attain illumination except through the abandonment of prejudices and the acquisition of the morals of the Kingdom.

Tablet to the Hague, p. 5

— *12* —

God maketh no distinction between the white and the black. If the hearts are pure both are acceptable unto Him. God is no respecter of persons on account of either color or race. All colors are acceptable to Him, be they white, black, or yellow. Inasmuch as all were created in the image of God, we must bring ourselves to realize that all embody divine possibilities. If you go into a garden and find all the flowers alike in form, species and color, the effect is wearisome to the eye. The garden is more beautiful when the flowers are many-colored and different; the variety lends charm and adornment. In a flock of doves some are white, some black, red, blue; yet they make no distinction among themselves. All are doves no matter what the color.

This variety in forms and colorings which is manifest in all the kingdoms is according to creative wisdom and has a divine purpose. Nevertheless, whether the creatures be all alike or all different should not be the cause of strife and quarreling among them. Especially why should man find cause for discord in the color or race of his fellow creature? No educated or illumined mind will allow that this differentiation and discord should exist or that there is any ground for it.

The Promulgation of Universal Peace, p. 112

13

All prejudices are against the will and plan of God. Consider, for instance, racial distinction and enmity. All humanity are the children of God; they belong to the same family, to the same original race. There can be no multiplicity of races, since all are the descendants of Adam. This signifies that racial assumption and distinction are nothing but superstition. In the estimate of God there are no English, French, Germans, Turkish or Persians. All these in the presence of God are equal; they are of one race and creation; God did not make these divisions. These distinctions have had their origin in man himself. Therefore, as they are against the plan and purpose of reality, they are false and imaginary. We are of one physical race, even as we are of one physical plan of material body—each endowed with two eyes, two ears, one head, two feet. Among the animals racial prejudice does not exist. Consider the doves; there is no distinction as to whether it is an oriental or an occidental dove. The sheep are all of one race; there is no assumption of distinction between an eastern and a western sheep. When they meet, they associate with perfect fellowship. . . . Is it reasonable or allowable that a racial prejudice which is not observed by the animal kingdom should be entertained by man?

The Promulgation of Universal Peace, p. 299

14

I pray that you attain to such a degree of good character and behavior that the names of black and white shall vanish. All shall be called human, just as the name for a flight of doves is dove. They are not called black and white. Likewise with other birds.

I hope that you attain to such a high degree—and this is impossible except through love. You must try to create love between yourselves; and this love does not come about unless you are grateful to the whites, and the whites are loving toward you, and endeavor to promote your advancement and enhance your honor. This will be the cause of love. Differences between black and white will be completely obliterated; indeed, ethnic and national differences will all disappear.

I am very happy to see you and thank God that this meeting is composed of people of both races and that both are gathered in perfect love and harmony. I hope this becomes the example of universal harmony and love until no title remains except that of humanity. Such a title demonstrates the perfection of the human world and is the cause of eternal glory and human happiness. I pray that you be with one another in utmost harmony and love and strive to enable each other to live in comfort.

The Promulgation of Universal Peace, p. 45

FROM THE WRITINGS OF SHOGHI EFFENDI

— *15* —

As to racial prejudice, the corrosion of which, for well nigh a century, has bitten into the fiber, and attacked the whole social structure of American society, it should be regarded as constituting the most vital and challenging issue confronting the Baha'i community at the present stage of its evolution. The ceaseless exertions which this issue of paramount importance calls for, the sacrifices it must impose, the care and vigilance it demands, the moral courage and fortitude it requires, the tact and sympathy it necessitates, invest this problem, which the American believers are still far from having satisfactorily resolved, with an urgency and importance that cannot be overestimated. White and Negro, high and low, young and old, whether newly converted to the Faith or not, all who stand identified with it must participate in, and lend their assistance, each according to his or her capacity, experience, and opportunities, to the common task of fulfilling the instructions, realizing the hopes, and following the example, of 'Abdu'l-Bahá. Whether colored or non-colored, neither race has the right, or can conscientiously claim, to be regarded as absolved from such an obligation, as having realized such hopes, or having faithfully followed such an example. A long and thorny road, beset with pitfalls, still remains untraveled, both by the white and the Negro exponents of the redeeming Faith of Bahá'u'lláh. On the distance they cover, and the manner in which they travel that road, must depend, to an extent which few among them can imagine, the operation of those intangible influences which are indispensable to the spiritual triumph of the American believers and the material success of their newly launched enterprise.

Let them call to mind, fearlessly and determinedly, the example and conduct of 'Abdu'l-Bahá while in their midst. Let them remember His courage, His genuine love, His informal and indiscriminating fellowship, His contempt for and impatience of criticism, tempered by His tact and wisdom. Let them revive and perpetuate the memory of those unforgettable and historic episodes and occasions on which He so strikingly demonstrated His keen sense of justice, His spontaneous sympathy for the downtrodden, His ever-abiding sense of the oneness of the human race, His overflowing love for its members, and His displeasure with those who dared to flout His wishes, to deride His methods, to challenge His principles, or to nullify His acts.

To discriminate against any race, on the ground of its being socially backward, politically immature, and numerically in a minority, is a flagrant violation of the spirit that animates the Faith of Baha'u'llah. The consciousness of any division or cleavage in its ranks is alien to its very purpose, principles, and ideals. Once its members have fully recognized the claim of its Author, and, by identifying themselves with its Administrative Order, accepted unreservedly the principles and laws embodied in its teachings, every differentiation of class, creed, or color must automatically be obliterated, and never be allowed, under any pretext, and however great the pressure of events or of public opinion, to reassert itself. If any discrimination is at all to be tolerated, it should be a discrimination not against, but rather in favor of the minority, be it racial or otherwise. Unlike the nations and peoples of the earth, be they of the East or of the West, democratic or authoritarian, communist or capitalist, whether belonging to the Old World or the New, who either ignore, trample upon, or extirpate, the racial, religious, or political minorities within the sphere of their jurisdiction, every organized community enlisted under the banner of Baha'u'llah should feel it to be its first and inescapable obligation to nurture, encourage, and safeguard every minority belonging to any faith, race, class, or nation within it. So great and vital is this principle that in such circumstances, as when an equal number of ballots have been cast in an election, or where the qualifications for any office are balanced as between the various races, faiths or nationalities within the community, priority should unhesitatingly be accorded the party representing the minority, and this for no other reason except to stimulate and encourage it, and afford it an opportunity to further the interests of the community. In the light of this principle, and bearing in mind the extreme desirability of having the minority elements participate and share responsibility in the conduct of Bahá'í activity, it should be the duty of every Bahá'í community so to arrange its affairs that in cases where individuals belonging to the divers minority elements within it are already qualified and fulfill the necessary requirements, Bahá'í representative institutions, be they Assemblies, conventions, conferences, or committees, may have represented on them as many of these divers elements, racial or otherwise, as possible. The adoption of such a course, and faithful adherence to it, would not only be a source of inspiration and encouragement to those elements that are numerically small and inadequately represented, but would demonstrate to the world at large the universality, and representative character of the Faith of Bahá'u'lláh, and the freedom of His followers from the taint of those prejudices which have already wrought such havoc in the domestic affairs, as well as the foreign relationships, of the nations.

Freedom from racial prejudice, in any of its forms, should, at such a time as this when an increasingly large section of the human race is falling a victim to its devastating ferocity, be adopted as the watchword of the entire body of the American believers, in whichever state they reside, in whatever circles they move, whatever their age, traditions, tastes, and habits. It should be consistently demonstrated in every phase of their activity and life, whether in the Baha'i community or outside it, in public or in private, formally as well as informally, individually as well as in their official capacity as organized groups, committees and Assemblies. It should be deliberately cultivated through the various and everyday opportunities, no matter how insignificant, that present themselves, whether in their homes, their business offices, their schools and colleges, their social parties and recreation grounds, their Baha'i meetings, conferences, conventions, summer schools and Assemblies. It should, above all else, become the keynote of the policy of that august body which, in its capacity as the national representative, and the director and coordinator of the affairs of the community, must set the example, and facilitate the application of such a vital principle to the lives and activities of those whose interests it safeguards and represents.

"O ye discerning ones!" Bahá'u'lláh has written, "Verily, the words which have descended from the heaven of the Will of God are the source of unity and harmony for the world. Close your eyes to racial differences, and welcome all with the light of oneness." "We desire but the good of the world and the happiness of the nations," He proclaims," . . . that all nations should become one in faith and all men as brothers; that the bonds of affection and unity between the sons of men should be strengthened; that diversity of religion should cease, and differences of race be annulled." "Bahá'u'lláh hath said, writes 'Abdu'l-Bahá, "that the various races of humankind lend a composite harmony and beauty of color to the whole. Let all associate, therefore, in this great human garden even as flowers grow and blend together side by side without discord or disagreement between them." "Bahá'u'lláh," 'Abdu'l-Bahá moreover has said, "once compared the colored people to the black pupil of the eye surrounded by the white. In this black pupil is seen the reflection of that which is before it, and through it the light of the spirit shineth forth."

"God," 'Abdu'l-Bahá Himself declares, "maketh no distinction between the white and the black. If the hearts are pure both are acceptable unto Him. God is no respecter of persons on account of either color or race. All colors are acceptable unto Him, be they white, black, or yellow. Inasmuch as all were created in the image of God, we must bring ourselves to realize that all embody divine possibilities." "In the estimation of God," He states, "all men are equal. There is no distinction or preference for any soul, in the realm of His justice and equity." "God did not make these divisions," He affirms; "these divisions have had their origin in man himself. Therefore, as they are against the plan and purpose of God they are false and imaginary." "In the estimation of God," He again affirms, "there is no distinction of color; all are one in the color and beauty of servitude to Him. Color is not important; the heart is all-important. It mattereth not what the exterior may be if the heart is pure and white within. God doth not behold differences of hue and complexion. He looketh at the hearts. He whose morals and virtues are praiseworthy is preferred in the presence of God; he who is devoted to the Kingdom is most beloved. In the realm of genesis and creation the question of color is of least importance." "Throughout the animal kingdom," He explains, "we do not find the creatures separated because of color. They recognize unity of species and oneness of kind. If we do not find color distinction drawn in a kingdom of lower intelligence and reason, how can it be justified among human beings, especially when we know that all have come from the same source and belong to the same household? In origin and intention of creation mankind is one. Distinctions of race and color have arisen afterward." "Man is endowed with superior reasoning power and the faculty of perception"; He further explains, "he is the manifestation of divine bestowals. Shall racial ideas prevail and obscure the creative purpose of unity in his kingdom?" "One of the important questions," He significantly remarks, "which affect the unity and the solidarity of mankind is the fellowship and equality of the white and colored races. Between these two races certain points of agreement and points of distinction exist which warrant just and mutual consideration. The points of contact are many. . . . In this country, the United States of America, patriotism is common to both races; all have equal rights to citizenship, speak one language, receive the blessings of the same civilization, and follow the precepts of the same religion. In fact numerous points of partnership and agreement exist between the two races, whereas the one point of distinction is that of color. Shall this, the least of all distinctions, be allowed to separate you as races and individuals?" "This variety in forms and coloring," He stresses, "which is manifest in all the kingdoms is according to creative Wisdom and hath a divine purpose." "The diversity in the human family," He claims, "should be the cause of love and harmony, as it is in music where many different notes blend together in the making of a perfect chord." "If you meet," is His admonition, "those of a different race and color from yourself, do not mistrust them, and withdraw yourself into your shell of conventionality, but rather be glad and show them kindness." "In the world of being," He testifies, "the meeting is blessed when the white and colored races meet together with infinite spiritual love and heavenly harmony. When such meetings are established, and the participants associate with each other with perfect love, unity and kindness, the angels of the

Kingdom praise them, and the Beauty of Bahá'u'lláh addresseth them, 'Blessed are ye! Blessed are ye!'" "When a gathering of these two races is brought about," He likewise asserts, "that assemblage will become the magnet of the Concourse on high, and the confirmation of the Blessed Beauty will surround it." "Strive earnestly," He again exhorts both races, "and put forth your greatest endeavor toward the accomplishment of this fellowship and the cementing of this bond of brotherhood between you. Such an attainment is not possible without will and effort on the part of each; from one, expressions of gratitude and appreciation; from the other, kindliness and recognition of equality. Each one should endeavor to develop and assist the other toward mutual advancement. . . . Love and unity will be fostered between you, thereby bringing about the oneness of mankind. For the accomplishment of unity between the colored and white will be an assurance of the world's peace." "I hope," He thus addresses members of the white race, "that ye may cause that down-trodden race to become glorious, and to be joined with the white race, to serve the world of man with the utmost sincerity, faithfulness, love, and purity. This opposition, enmity, and prejudice among the white race and the colored cannot be effaced except through faith, assurance, and the teachings of the Blessed Beauty." "This question of the union of the white and the black is very important," He warns, "for if it is not realized, erelong great difficulties will arise, and harmful results will follow." "If this matter remaineth without change," is yet another warning, "enmity will be increased day by day, and the final result will be hardship and may end in bloodshed."

A tremendous effort is required by both races if their outlook, their manners, and conduct are to reflect, in this darkened age, the spirit and teachings of the Faith of Bahá'u'lláh. Casting away once and for all the fallacious doctrine of racial superiority, with all its attendant evils, confusion, and miseries, and welcoming and encouraging the intermixture of races, and tearing down the barriers that now divide them, they should each endeavor, day and night, to fulfill their particular responsibilities in the common task which so urgently faces them. Let them, while each is attempting to contribute its share to the solution of this perplexing problem, call to mind the warnings of 'Abdu'l-Bahá, and visualize, while there is yet time, the dire consequences that must follow if this challenging and unhappy situation that faces the entire American nation is not definitely remedied.

Let the white make a supreme effort in their resolve to contribute their share to the solution of this problem, to abandon once for all their usually inherent and at times subconscious sense of superiority, to correct their tendency towards revealing a patronizing attitude towards the members of the other race, to persuade them through their intimate, spontaneous and informal association with them of the genuineness of their friendship and the sincerity of their intentions, and to master their impatience of any lack of responsiveness on the part of a people who have received, for so long a period, such grievous and slow-healing wounds. Let the Negroes, through a corresponding effort on their part, show by every means in their power the warmth of their response, their readiness to forget the past, and their ability to wipe out every trace of suspicion that may still linger in their hearts and minds. Let neither think that the solution of so vast a problem is a matter that exclusively concerns the other. Let neither think that such a problem can either easily or immediately be resolved. Let neither think that they can wait confidently for the solution of this problem until the initiative has been taken, and the favorable circumstances created, by agencies that stand outside the orbit of their Faith. Let neither think that anything short of genuine love, extreme patience, true humility, consummate tact, sound initiative, mature wisdom, and deliberate, persistent, and prayerful effort, can succeed in blotting out the stain which this patent evil has left on the fair name of their common country. Let them rather believe, and be firmly convinced, that on their mutual understanding, their amity, and sustained cooperation, must depend, more than on any other force or organization operating outside the circle of their Faith, the deflection of that dangerous course so greatly feared by 'Abdu'l-Bahá, and the materialization of the hopes He cherished for their joint contribution to the fulfillment of that country's glorious destiny.

The Advent of Divine Justice, pp. 33-41.

FROM LETTERS WRITTEN BY THE UNIVERSAL HOUSE OF
JUSTICE

— 16 —

A moment of historic portent has arrived for your nation as the conscience of its citizenry has stirred, creating possibilities for marked social change. It holds significance not only for the destiny of America anticipated in the Sacred Writings, but also for the mission entrusted to your community by the hand of 'Abdu'l-Bahá, who cherished you dearly and called you to a path of sacrifice and high endeavor. We are pleased to see that, led by your National and Local Spiritual Assemblies, you are seizing opportunities— whether those thrust upon you by current circumstances or those derived from your systematic labors in the wider society—to play your part, however humble, in the effort to remedy the ills of your nation. We ardently pray that the American people will grasp the possibilities of this moment to create a consequential reform of the social order that will free it from the pernicious effects of racial prejudice and will hasten the attainment of a just, diverse, and united society that can increasingly manifest the oneness of the human family.

Sadly, however, your nation's history reveals that any significant progress toward racial equality has invariably been met by countervailing processes, overt or covert, that served to undermine the advances achieved and to reconstitute the forces of oppression by other means. Thus, whatever the immediate outcome of contemporary events, you need not be deterred, for you are cognizant of the "long and thorny road, beset with pitfalls" described by the Guardian that still lies ahead. Your commitment to tread this road with determination and insight, drawing upon what you have learned in recent years about translating Bahá'u'lláh's teachings into reality, will have to be sustained until the time, anticipated by Shoghi Effendi, when you will have contributed your decisive share to the eradication of racial prejudice from the fabric of your nation.

The principles and exhortations that guide your steps are well known to you from the writings of 'Abdu'l-Bahá and Shoghi Effendi. The concepts and approaches for social transformation developed in the current series of Plans that can be utilized to promote race unity in the context of community building, social action, and involvement in the discourses of society have been set out in our messages. Every believer, as the promulgator of Bahá'u'lláh's central principle of the oneness of humanity, should deeply meditate upon it and weigh its demanding implications for the profound alteration of thought and action required at this time. "The American Bahá'í Community, the leaven destined to leaven the whole," the Guardian admonished, cannot hope "to either escape the trials with which this nation is confronted, nor claim to be wholly immune from the evils that stain its character." "A tremendous effort is required by both races if their outlook, their manners, and conduct are to reflect, in this darkened age, the spirit and teachings of the Faith of Bahá'u'lláh," he also stated. "Let neither think that the solution of so vast a problem is a matter that exclusively concerns the other. Let neither think that such a problem can either easily or immediately be resolved." "Each one should endeavor to develop and assist the other toward mutual advancement," 'Abdu'l-Bahá explained. "Love and unity will be fostered between you, thereby bringing about the oneness of mankind."

Racism is a profound deviation from the standard of true morality. It deprives a portion of humanity of the opportunity to cultivate and express the full range of their capability and to live a meaningful and flourishing life, while blighting the progress of the rest of humankind. It cannot be rooted out by contest and conflict. It must be supplanted by the establishment of just relationships among individuals, communities, and institutions of society that will uplift all and will not designate anyone as "other". The change required is not merely social and economic, but above all moral and spiritual. Within the context of the framework governing your activities, it is necessary to carefully examine the forces unfolding around you to determine where your energies might reinforce the most promising initiatives, what you should avoid, and how you might lend a distinctive contribution. It is not possible for you to effect the transformation envisioned by Bahá'u'lláh merely by adopting the perspectives, practices, concepts, criticisms, and language of contemporary society. Your approach, instead, will be distinguished by maintaining a humble posture of learning, weighing alternatives in the light of His teachings, consulting to harmonize differing views and shape collective action, and marching forward with unbreakable unity in serried lines.

Ultimately, the power to transform the world is effected by love, love originating from the relationship with the divine, love ablaze among members of a community, love extended without restriction to every human being. This divine love, ignited by the Word of God, is disseminated by enkindled souls through intimate conversations that create new susceptibilities in human hearts, open minds to moral persuasion, and loosen the hold of biased norms and social systems so that they can gradually take on a new form in keeping with the requirements of humanity's age of maturity. You are channels for this divine love; let it flow through you to all who cross your path. Infuse it into every neighborhood and social space in which you move to build capacity to canalize the society-building power of Bahá'u'lláh's Revelation. There can be no rest until the destined outcome is achieved.

Ahead of you lie times of trial and promise, of hardship and progress, of anguish and joy. Under all conditions, the Master is your solace and support. For those who aspire to lasting change, His example guides the way—tactful and wise in His approach, penetrating in utterance, indiscriminating in fellowship, unfailing in sympathy for the downtrodden, courageous in conduct, persevering in action, imperturbable in the face of tests, unwavering in His keen sense of justice. And to all who arise to emulate Him, He offers this unfailing assurance: "that which is confirmed is the oneness of the world of humanity. Every soul who serveth this oneness will undoubtedly be assisted and confirmed."

To the Bahá'ís of the United States, 22 July 2020

— *17* —

The Nine Year Plan is now in motion. The outstanding achievements that you bring to this new stage of the Divine Plan place your community in the very front ranks of the worldwide Bahá'í community. Before you stretches a path of great possibilities, and we are confident that you are primed to surpass all you have to this point attained.

Your country is blessed with remarkable ethnic and cultural

diversity. How happy we have been over the years to witness the receptivity of its peoples to the Teachings of Bahá'u'lláh. Yet, alas, your nation has time and again suffered from conflict among some of its peoples. As a part of Congolese society, you are, of course, not immune to the forces that generate and drive conflict. What this demands is vigilance by all the believers in ensuring that divisions, especially those related to ethnicity, do not take root in your community. Such divisions can impede your efforts to develop your community and to foster the spiritual and material progress of your nation. Your duty as Bahá'ís is to act as true champions of the oneness of humankind, and to promote unity in your communities and in the life of your nation. It is about this vital duty that we wish to address you.

Each of the hundreds of ethnic groups in your country has a long history, and each has gradually been shaped and reshaped by encounters with other groups and cultures over periods both of peace and of conflict. Such a pattern is, of course, not unique to the Democratic Republic of the Congo. It is the story of the peoples of the world, a reality on which the Bahá'í conception of history sheds much light. As a distinct organic unit, humanity has passed through evolutionary stages that are similar to the stages of infancy and childhood in the lives of its individual members. The divisions and conflicts that have marked relationships among and within various peoples are tendencies of humanity's childhood. Inexorably, however, humanity has been moving forward along the path of its maturation. On this path, it has, from one age to the next, received impetus from successive Divine Revelations sent by God to progressively educate and civilize it. Humanity is now in the concluding period of its turbulent adolescence and is going through a period of transition. Standing at the threshold of a long-awaited coming of age, its needs are no longer served by the ideas and behaviours of prior stages.

Bahá'u'lláh has appeared to humanity in this period of its adolescence, when it is in need of maturation. As you are well aware, He has provided the means for establishing the unity of humankind, the hallmark of a mature world. What will bind the hearts of all people together is the power of the Word of God. That Word has generative power which in every age has provided the means for refining human character and reordering human affairs.

The mission of the Bahá'ís is to learn to apply the Revelation of Bahá'u'lláh in their individual and collective lives and in the life of their society. Through well-ordered efforts and in collaboration with many others who are dedicated to bettering the world, Bahá'ís bring the principles suited to humanity's age of maturity to bear on the conditions of the world's peoples. They strive for the transformation of the inner and outer realities of human life, and for the cultivation of spiritual and social conditions that will give rise to a new kind of people and a new society founded on unity.

Bahá'ís undertake this work with instruments and means that are conducive to creating a unified world. They are ever conscious that unity is not only the goal they seek but the primary means for creating a new and mature society. They thus labour together in "serried lines", "one locked to the next, each supporting his fellows". They are equipped with pure intent, righteous motives, sincere aims, and faithful hearts. They "associate with all the peoples and kindreds of the earth with joy and radiance", with the assurance that "consorting with people hath promoted and will continue to promote unity and concord". They strive to rid their actions of any animosity or hatred and seek always to "hold fast to the cord of kindliness and tender mercy". They are above all cognizant that "the religion of God is for love and unity" and should never be made the cause of enmity or dissension, and that "the means of order" should never become "the cause of confusion", or "the instrument of union an occasion for discord".

It is only as a united community that you can thrive as promoters of the oneness of humanity. It is important, then, that you continue to enrich your understanding of how obstacles to unity appear in society. We would like to discuss two such obstacles: the distortion of human identity and the spread of prejudice, in particular, ethnic prejudice.

———— ⌘ ————

At the heart of the divisions in society today is a crisis of identity. The way people think about who they are and how they see their place in the world determine how they relate to others and what they regard as their individual and collective purpose. For

Bahá'ís, it is the Manifestation of God, the Voice of God to the world, who defines human nature and purpose. Bahá'u'lláh describes the purpose of human life as essentially spiritual in nature. An individual's true self is to be found in the powers of the soul, which has the capacity to know God and to reflect His attributes. The soul has no gender, no ethnicity, no race. God sees no differences among human beings except in relation to the conscious effort of each individual to purify his or her soul and to express its full powers. In God's sight, all human beings are as one and have the common duty of knowing and worshiping Him and contributing to advancing civilization. This truth is directly related to another—that humanity is one family. A loving Lord has "created all humanity from the same stock". He has "decreed that all shall belong to the same household". "Since We have created you all from one same substance", Bahá'u'lláh has stated, "it is incumbent on you to be even as one soul, to walk with the same feet, eat with the same mouth and dwell in the same land, that from your inmost being, by your deeds and actions, the signs of oneness and the essence of detachment may be made manifest."

The powers of the human soul have throughout history and across the planet been manifested in many forms of custom, knowledge, and culture. This diversity endows the human family with richness. Just as differently coloured flowers enrich a garden, diversity gives society natural beauty and strength. "Consider", 'Abdu'l-Bahá explains, "the flowers of a garden: though differing in kind, colour, form and shape, yet, inasmuch as they are refreshed by the waters of one spring, revived by the breath of one wind, invigorated by the rays of one sun, this diversity increaseth their charm, and addeth unto their beauty." "In like manner," He adds, "when divers shades of thought, temperament and character, are brought together under the power and influence of one central agency, the beauty and glory of human perfection will be revealed and made manifest." Unity in diversity, not uniformity, is thus the watchword of Bahá'u'lláh's Teachings.

But consider what a grave obstacle to the unity of the human family is presented by failure to understand the truth of its essential oneness! Any sense of unity that comes from the shared identity of a group becomes the basis of contest with those perceived as "other". Humanity is split into competing interest groups, many locked in a fight for dominance. Conceptions of conflicting interests inhibit the collective capacity to transform social conditions and address challenges for the benefit of all. In the religious, social, political, and economic spheres of life, conflict driven by narrow self-interest is deemed natural and inevitable. Rivalry between groups harms all, obstructs justice, and suppresses the potentialities of individuals and groups, whose contributions are necessary for the betterment of society.

The responsibility Bahá'ís bear—the work you are carrying out in your localities, clusters, and nation—is to assist all peoples to recognize their shared identity as members of one human family and thus join together in building spiritually and materially prosperous societies that manifest unity in diversity. Every people has a part to play in this enterprise. Each brings the best aspects of their culture to broader social interactions and places them at the service of all, even as they discard aspects unconducive to the common good. In this light, the diversity of ethnic origins and traditions that distinguish the peoples of your country is a treasure that enriches your nation and the world. What a blessing is theirs—each and all—when they widen their loyalty to embrace the best interests of their entire nation and the whole of humanity so that they can, as members of one family, prosper and flourish.

———————— ◦✍︎◦ ————————

The crisis of identity is directly related to the spread of prejudice. Today, prejudices of all sorts are surging around the world, infecting the consciousness of millions and despoiling them of their energies. They are polarizing societies at a time when unity is most vital to resolving local, national, and global challenges that seem intractable.

The statements in the writings of the Faith about the harm that prejudice inflicts on individuals and on society are most emphatic. 'Abdu'l-Bahá has stated that human beings are degraded when they become captives of their own illusions and suppositions. Prejudice stains the human spirit, debases both its perpetrator and its victim, obscures perception and understanding, and prevents the achievement of that lofty standard of justice proclaimed in the writings to "see with thine own eyes and not through the eyes of others," and to "know of thine own knowledge and not through the knowledge of thy neighbour." 'Abdu'l-Bahá has also made it clear that prejudice is "destructive of the human edifice", "a destroyer of the foundations of the world of humanity", and the cause of "the world's sickness". Until prejudice is removed, "the world of humanity will not and cannot attain peace, prosperity and composure". "The world of humanity cannot be saved from the darkness of nature and cannot attain illumination except through the abandonment of prejudices and the acquisition of the morals of the Kingdom."

Our particular concern here, as we have stated, is ethnic prejudice. To distrust, fear, hate, or discriminate against another person or a whole group on the basis of ethnicity is a spiritual disease. It is also a scourge that infects social structures and causes instability. In this light, eradicating ethnic prejudice requires transformation at the level of both the individual and the social environment. "We cannot segregate the human heart from the environment outside us", Shoghi Effendi stated in a letter written on his behalf, "and say that once one of these is reformed everything will be improved. Man is organic with the world. His inner life moulds the environment and is itself also deeply affected by it. The one acts upon the other and every abiding change in the life of man is the result of these mutual reactions."

For the individual, striving to be free from ethnic prejudice is a profound spiritual duty that no one who claims to be a loyal follower of Bahá'u'lláh can neglect. To discriminate against anyone because of ethnicity grievously violates the spirit that animates the Faith. "If any discrimination is at all to be tolerated," Shoghi Effendi stated, "it should be a discrimination not against, but rather in favour of the minority". Whatever the strength of public opinion, a Bahá'í should never act in a way that would alienate anyone. "Let them see no one as their enemy, or as wishing them ill," 'Abdu'l-Bahá states, "but think of all humankind as their friends; regarding the alien as an intimate, the stranger as a companion, staying free of prejudice, drawing no lines."

An individual's efforts in this respect must begin with earnest striving to develop attributes of the soul such as love, truthfulness, kindness, justice, and generosity; to purify the heart of selfishness, envy, and hate; and to align the mind with Bahá'u'lláh's principles of unity. By striving to rid his or her thoughts, words, and actions of ethnic bias, an individual upholds his or her own nobility and the nobility of all of God's children. Freedom from prejudice must then manifest itself in all aspects of an individual's life—in private and public life, in the Bahá'í community, and in the wider society. The home environment must be free of attitudes, tendencies, expressions, and associations that give room for prejudice. In the Bahá'í community, God forbid that a loyal believer's participation in the electoral processes of the Faith be swayed by narrow ethnic interests or that service on committees, agencies, and institutions be tainted by partiality and favouritism. In society, a believer's freedom from prejudice must be evident in all the social spaces he or she enters—the school, the workplace, the cultural association, the professional organization. A believer's duty at all times is to demonstrate the unifying power of Bahá'u'lláh's Teachings by associating with diverse peoples with a spacious heart, an all-embracing love, and a spirit of true friendship. As was 'Abdu'l-Bahá's injunction, "Let those who meet you know, without your proclaiming the fact, that you are indeed a Bahá'í."

As for the social environment, ethnic prejudice can pervade many aspects of collective life and, at its worst, be manifest in recurring cycles of violent conflict. Ethnic prejudice is often driven or exacerbated by prevalent negative social factors, and the friends must seek to obtain a mature understanding of these factors if they are to contribute meaningfully to eradicating its effects. Consider, for instance, the effects of ignorance and how it blinds people to the truths that all human beings share the same spiritual essence, are members of one human family, and are inhabitants of one common homeland. Where people are uninformed of the historical processes that have shaped their society, they can tenaciously cling to divisive identities that may have had their roots in an oppressive past. Political partitions between or within countries, which are but human inventions, become bases for the irrational distrust and fear of other groups. Consider also the consequences of a tendency to blindly imitate and uncritically perpetuate divisive ways of thinking, speaking, and relating. Skewed historical accounts transmitted by one generation to the next are employed to propagate narrow notions of belonging, to advance claims of exceptionalism, to stir old rivalries, or to stress past events that evoke a sense of victimhood. Language is flippantly used to entrench negative stereotypes that stigmatize and malign others. Consider as well how at the service of narrow self-interest—whether political or economic—divisions are stoked, rivalries started, and conflicts sustained, how, in essence, ethnicity is employed as an instrument in pursuit of political power and economic advantage. Consider, too, how materialism widens the extremes of wealth and poverty and how economic injustice produces rifts that intensify prejudice, even among similarly marginalized peoples. Competition for limited resources sullies personal and collective motives and generates hostilities and jealousies that embitter relationships.

These are among the factors that create social environments in which ethnic prejudice proliferates. All well-meaning people have a duty to increase their consciousness of such factors and to strengthen their capacity to counteract them. The influence of culture also has to be borne in mind. Each culture has many salutary elements that are conducive to promoting unity in diversity, which must be reinforced, as well as negative aspects that contribute to breeding prejudice, which must be gradually abandoned. Meaningful interactions among people hailing from different human groups foster an environment within which advances in culture can occur. To retain and promote customs and traditions that generate animosity is a grave obstacle to the betterment of society. A Bahá'í community is robbed of its ability to promote unity in diversity if the friends, knowingly or unknowingly, reproduce in their interactions and their association with society the same tendencies that foment prejudice.

———————⟨✖⟩———————

What is the work before you then? How are you to strengthen patterns of interaction that promote unity in diversity and eliminate prevalent social factors that drive prejudice? How is this objective related to your current efforts to build vibrant communities and, more broadly, to contribute to the spiritual and material well-being of your society?

Shoghi Effendi called on the friends to "scale nobler heights of heroism as humanity plunges into greater depths of despair, degradation, dissension and distress". The global Plans seek to build capacity in every human group to counter negative social forces by contributing to social well-being through the application of the teachings of the Faith. As the Plans steadily unfold, their processes will gradually realize their potential to disable every instrument devised by humanity over the long period of its childhood for one group to oppress another and for the perpetuation of conflict and contention. This is central to the work you are carrying out within your own communities. Your efforts in the fields of community building, social action, and public discourse represent ways of awakening the energies latent in the human soul and channelling them towards the betterment of society.

Your endeavours to reach different social groups with the message of the Faith foster profound interethnic and intercultural association. They make cooperation and mutual assistance among people of many backgrounds a distinctive characteristic of Bahá'í community life. You seek, in this, to demonstrate that vital Bahá'í attitude of being truly outward looking, sincerely open to all, and resolutely inclusive. Your attention to strengthening capacity to study the writings of the Faith enables ever-larger numbers to forge relationships that reflect Bahá'í standards and principles. This reinforces in all participants the desire and ability to offer acts of disinterested service to society and to purify their motives as they learn to sacrifice for the progress and well-being of all. Your dedication to a mode of operation centred on ongoing study, consultation, action, and reflection helps to free individuals and communities from blind imitation and to anchor unfolding efforts in learning to establish "new bases for human happiness". The energies you give to the spiritual education of children and the spiritual empowerment of junior youth help the younger generations lay the foundations of a noble character, shield them from the taint of prejudice, and incline their burgeoning powers towards service to society. The focus you place on the family transforms that fundamental unit of society into a space where young people can imbibe the spirit of unity and shun all dispositions that breed division. Your endeavours to build capacity for applying spiritual principles and scientific knowledge to the improvement of social and economic conditions help populations address economic injustice through unified action and without resort to conflict. Your contributions in multiple spaces where conversations on various social problems occur strengthen collective capacity for elevated dialogue and help diverse actors achieve unity of thought and action by drawing on insights from the Bahá'í teachings and experience. The centrality you give to consultation increases capacity for collective investigation of truth, frees decision-making processes from contest and adversarial tendencies, and enables people from diverse backgrounds to transcend differences and harmonize perspectives. The electoral and administrative processes you foster shape thought and conduct that free leadership and governance from self-interest and the associated corruption. By striving to broaden the base of participation in all aspects of the life of your communities, you cultivate conditions in which individuals from various social groups honour their common humanity, recognize their mutual interests, and envision their shared future. Such participation strengthens social bonds as souls serve side by side for the betterment of society. Whether large or small, your community-building efforts are directed at raising the nucleus and pattern of a new World Order by establishing the kind of relationships called for by Bahá'u'lláh. And emerging among all who are labouring together is a language that elevates all and maligns none, a language with the potency to bind hearts with the indissoluble bond of love and the power to unite minds in common pursuit of a society that can truly be as a garden bursting with flowers of every form, every colour, every fragrance. It is in all these ways that you are creating new communities that can serve as a model and relationships that enable you to act as leaven in the life of your nation.

———————⌒∞⌒———————

Beloved friends in that great African nation! We know that the conditions of societal conflict under which you labour are at times disruptive and dispiriting. Your brothers and sisters in many other lands also face similar conditions. Though it may sometimes appear as if hope for a truly united society grows dimmer day after day as conflicts borne of prejudice recur and resurge, your mission must remain ever clear, your outlook ever confident, your dedication ever firm. You possess the means for unifying thousands upon thousands of hearts. You who are raising the song of unity in diversity must be, in word and deed, its very emblems. If your actions mirror the tendencies widespread in society, if you are negligent of the fundamentals of your belief, what then will be left? The salt will have lost its savour. Set aside all obstacles, mental and otherwise, and thus deliver to a loving Lord during these nine years a true victory for the oneness of humanity.

In closing, we now address the youth: The future is in your hands. Make no mistake, you are raising an edifice that will be a haven for your peoples upon the foundations your mothers and your fathers have laid. Continued progress will depend on your dedication to building true unity and on the extent to which you strengthen your practice of those spiritual disciplines enjoined by Bahá'u'lláh that help you polish the mirrors of your hearts to reflect the attributes of God. We hope that you will foster among yourselves enduring spiritual bonds that resist the forces of prejudice. Let the example of 'Abdu'l-Bahá be your guide—how He lived His life as a daily sacrifice to the cause of the oneness of humanity, how He embraced with selfless love all people who crossed His path, how He saw reflected in each soul the image of a loving God. So, too, are you to see all your compatriots. "In this illumined age", He stated, "that which is confirmed is the oneness of the world of humanity. Every soul who serveth this oneness will undoubtedly be assisted and confirmed." We cherish the hope that in your efforts to find life partners you will resist every influence to give primacy to ethnicity, that you will build homes in which every soul would be welcome, and that you will raise children who will become champions of oneness. We are confident that in the life of your nation, you will shine as well-wishers of all, as servants of all, as unifiers of all. Let your deeds write the next chapter of your country's history, one that is free of prejudice and conflict. Thus will your peoples, each as a powerful tributary, stream into one mighty river, whose surging waters will gush forth into the ocean of one human family.

We will supplicate the Blessed Beauty at the Sacred Threshold of His Shrine that He may bind the peoples of your much cherished nation ever more firmly in love.

To the Followers of Bahá'u'lláh
in the Democratic Republic of the Congo, 1 November 2022

LETTERS WRITTEN ON BEHALF
OF THE UNIVERSAL HOUSE OF JUSTICE

— *18* —

After a decade and a half of systematic effort, a coherent pattern of activity that advances the growth and development of the Bahá'í community and its greater involvement in the life of society has emerged. The current stage of progress and the challenges that lie immediately ahead are summarized in the Riḍván 2010 and 28 December 2010 messages. From this perspective, it is possible to see how the challenge of addressing racial prejudice is an integral part of three broad areas of activity in which the Bahá'í world is currently engaged: expansion and consolidation, social action, and participation in the discourses of society.

The pattern of spiritual and social life taking shape in clusters that involves study circles, children's classes, junior youth groups, devotional meetings, home visits, teaching efforts, and reflection meetings, as well as Holy Day observances, Nineteen Day Feasts, and other gatherings, provides abundant opportunities for engagement, experience, consultation, and learning that will lead to change in personal and collective understanding and action. Issues of prejudice of race, class, and color will inevitably arise as the friends reach out to diverse populations, especially in the closely knit context of neighborhoods. There, every activity can take a form most suited to the culture and interests of the population, so that new believers can be quickened and confirmed in a nurturing and familiar environment, until they are able to offer their share to the resolution of the challenges faced by a growing Bahá'í community. For this is not a process that some carry out on behalf of others who are passive recipients—the mere extension of a congregation and invitation to paternalism—but one in which an ever-increasing number of souls recognize and take responsibility for the transformation of humanity set in motion by Bahá'u'lláh. In an environment of love and trust born of common belief, practice, and mission, individuals of different races will have the intimate connection of heart and mind upon which mutual understanding and change depend. As a result of their training and deepening, a growing number of believers will draw insights from the Writings to sensitively and effectively address issues of racial prejudice that arise within their personal lives and families, among community members, and in social settings and the workplace. As programs of growth advance and the scope and intensity of activities grow, the friends will be drawn into participation in conversations and, in time, initiatives for social action at the grassroots where issues pertaining to freedom from prejudice naturally emerge, whether directly or indirectly. And, at the national level, the National Assembly will guide, through its Office of External Affairs, the engagement of the Faith with other agencies and individuals in the discourse pertaining to race unity.

You indicate that some friends wonder whether the Guardian's statement characterizing racial prejudice as "the most vital and challenging issue confronting the Bahá'í community at the present stage of its evolution" still applies to the racial situation in the United States, since it was written so long ago. The House of Justice has determined that it is not productive to approach the issue in this manner, as it gives rise to an implicit and false dichotomy that, either what the Guardian said is no longer important, or it is so important that it must be addressed before or apart from all other concerns. Yet, the situation is infinitely more complex. The American nation is much more diverse than in 1938, and the friends cannot be concerned only with relations between black and white, essential as they are. The expressions of racial prejudice have transmuted into forms that are multifaceted, less blatant and more intricate, and thus more intractable. So too, the American Bahá'í community has evolved significantly and is no longer at the same stage of its development; it faces a wider range of challenges but also possesses greater capabilities. The House of Justice stated that the principles Shoghi Effendi brought to the attention of the American believers more than seventy years ago are relevant today, and they will continue to be relevant to future generations. It is obvious, however, that the "long and thorny road, beset with pitfalls" upon which the friends must tread, will take them through an ever-changing landscape that requires that they adapt their approaches to varying circumstances.

In the 28 December message, the House of Justice explained that "A small community, whose members are united by their shared beliefs, characterized by their high ideals, proficient in managing their affairs and tending to their needs, and perhaps engaged in several humanitarian projects—a community such as this, prospering but at a comfortable distance from the reality experienced by the masses of humanity, can never hope to serve as a pattern for restructuring the whole of society." Even if such a community were to focus the entirety of its resources on the problem of racial prejudice, even if it were able to heal itself to some extent of that cancerous affliction, in the face of such a monumental social challenge the impact would be inconsequential. Therefore, the friends must effectively assess the forces at work in their society and, beginning in neighborhoods and clusters, contribute their share to the process of learning and systematization which, as their numbers, knowledge, and influence grow, will transform their lives, families, and communities. Only if the efforts to eradicate the bane of prejudice are coherent with the full range of the community's affairs, only if they arise naturally within the systematic pattern of expansion, community building, and involvement with society, will the American believers expand their capacity, year after year and decade after decade, to make their mark on their community and society and contribute to the high aim set for the Bahá'ís by 'Abdu'l-Bahá to eliminate racial prejudice from the face of the earth.

> Letter to an individual, 10 April 2011,
> in *Framework for Action*, pp. 280-282.

— *19* —

Surely, racial prejudice has for too long stained the fabric of life in the United States, and although the Bahá'í community has made enormous strides in the past century, like in so many other aspects of the Teachings, the response of the believers to this challenge has not yet reached the expectations 'Abdu'l-Bahá held for them. While Shoghi Effendi clearly expressed that the solution to this problem rests with both races, it cannot be denied that any failure or lessening of effort in redressing the problem within the framework for the social and administrative affairs of the community has its most immediate and negative consequences on the minority, as the majority can lapse into the unconscious state the Guardian warned them against. The House of Justice well appreciates that, for a Bahá'í, the injuries arising from one's interactions with a fellow believer can be especially painful.

The guidance provided to the friends by the beloved Guardian and the Universal House of Justice offers a clear way forward. As you know, Shoghi Effendi, in his masterful discourse in *The Advent of Divine Justice*, gives African American and white Bahá'ís detailed instructions as to their respective responsibilities in combating racial prejudice. "A tremendous effort", he emphasized, "is required by both races if their outlook, their manners, and conduct are to reflect, in this darkened age, the spirit and teachings of the Faith of Bahá'u'lláh." "Let neither think", he added, "that such a problem can either easily or immediately be resolved." Each person, of whatever race or background, was called upon to take the initiative and not allow what he perceives to be the shortcomings of his fellow believers to be the cause of his becoming apathetic or vindictive. By responding to the situation within the spiritual framework the Guardian has devised, one's actions may be imbued with the spirit of the Faith, thus making them potent instruments for effecting a change in the hearts of those who have inherited attitudes tainted by racial prejudice.

Beyond this spiritual orientation to combatting racial prejudice with which the friends in the United States are well familiar, the House of Justice has in recent years attempted to bring to the attention of those who long to eradicate the blight of racism—and especially the African American believers—the potentialities for transformation inherent in the systematic implementation of the instruments and methods of the current series of Plans.... As the friends pursue their efforts to promote growth and community building, social action, and involvement in the discourses of society, they will over time work increasingly with other well-meaning people to eliminate these and other problems that have so bedeviled the world. A profound illustration of the possibilities this approach holds is found in the video *Frontiers of Learning*, commissioned by the House of Justice and available on the website www.bahai.org/frontiers. It describes how the translation of the teachings into processes of community building in some of the most advanced clusters is beginning to address deep-seated social ills. An example cited is the Bihar Sharif cluster of India, where the centuries-old oppressive caste system is gradually being dismantled at the grassroots. As the video shows, communities are learning to mix without regard to caste, and a mother states with profound conviction that she will never tell her child into which caste he was born so that he will feel neither inferior nor superior to another soul. The House of Justice longs to hear of bold action being taken by the friends in the United States, who, by implementing the essential activities of the Five Year Plan and utilizing the spiritually transformative power of the training institute, begin to uproot racial prejudice in their neighborhoods.

'Abdu'l-Bahá made it clear that those who steadfastly strive to promote the oneness of humanity will endure hardship and injustice, and He taught that to be wronged and oppressed in the path of God is a divine gift, for it is a characteristic of the Manifestations of God. "And since the Ancient Beauty was exposed by day and night on the field of martyrdom," He counseled, "let us in our turn labor hard, and hear and ponder the counsels of God; let us fling away our lives, and renounce our brief and numbered days. Let us turn our eyes away from empty fantasies of this world's divergent forms, and serve instead this preeminent purpose, this grand design." You are encouraged to take heart from the Master's assurance that racial prejudice will one day be eliminated from the face of the earth, although as the Guardian explained, the road to be travelled will be "long and thorny" and "beset with pitfalls". In summoning us to the great work of creating anew the world, Bahá'u'lláh exhorts us to adhere to a standard of conduct which He, Himself, so nobly exemplified:

Adorn thyself with My virtues, in such wise that should anyone stretch forth the hand of oppression against thee, thou wouldst neither take notice nor contend with him. Leave him to the judgment of thy Lord, the All-Powerful, the Almighty, the Self-Subsisting, and be thou long-suffering under all conditions. By God! This is one of Mine attributes, though none but the sincere are apprised of it. Know thou then that the patient sighs of the oppressed are dearer to God than all deeds, could ye but comprehend it. Be patient in whatsoever may befall thee, and put thy trust in God, thy Lord, in all thine affairs. He, verily, doth suffice thee against the harm inflicted by all that have been and shall be, and doth protect thee within the shelter of His Cause and the stronghold of His custody.

From a letter to an individual, 27 March 2014

— 20 —

The House of Justice appreciates your thoughtful comments and admires your unflagging efforts over many years to address the challenge of racism in your nation, particularly at a time of its overt resurgence in a manner that would justifiably give rise to despair even in the stoutest heart. However discouraging the present events, however outrageous the injustices laid bare, however intractable the problem appears, such fresh evidences of this pernicious blight on American society can come as no surprise to those friends well informed of 'Abdu'l-Bahá's dire warnings as well as Shoghi Effendi's trenchant analysis anticipating the ultimate eradication of this evil tendency from the lives and the hearts of their fellow citizens. How much more must people endure in the years ahead? The current polarization in American society makes constructive dialogue and action ever more elusive. Even those fair-minded individuals who long to free themselves and their society from this problem—surely a vast portion of the nation—are paralyzed and divided by their divergent views, unable to create the unity necessary to advance along the path of constructive change.

It is in this context that the friends must understand their sacred obligation and the possibilities that lie before them. As you have observed, since the time of 'Abdu'l-Bahá's visit to the United States Bahá'ís have, whether individually or collectively, by themselves or in collaboration with others, been continually involved in diverse efforts to address prejudice and racism and build bonds and practices of racial accord. Such efforts, though sincere and even sacrificial, have yet to be raised to a level of systematic endeavor necessary for profound and lasting social change. Enclosed for your consideration is a copy of a letter written on behalf of the House of Justice to an individual believer concerning how the framework for action of the Plan offers precisely the vision and practical means by which Bahá'ís can, as their efforts are pursued in a learning mode, fulfill the high expectations the Guardian held for the American believers to help uproot the foundations of racism in your country. An extract is also provided from another letter which, in response to questions about climate change, offers guidance about how Bahá'ís can effectively participate in discourses about pressing social concerns.

Among the important lessons garnered over the past two decades is that, by focusing on insights derived from the most advanced and successful activities rather than by focusing on shortcomings and weaknesses, the community can come to understand what constitutes effective action and learn to disseminate the knowledge gained. Another lesson is how to approach the development of human resources in a manner that can efficiently multiply efforts and empower those who were previously left on the margins, or were otherwise unengaged, to become protagonists of a process of community building and social change. Therefore, it is not necessary at this time to propagate in the community a separate program centered on addressing racial prejudice before progress is possible, nor is there a need to remove one by one all the obstacles you describe before dynamic efforts can be established in a single community or neighborhood that can, once proven to be effective, be widely replicated. Consider, for example, the development of the junior youth spiritual empowerment program. Years ago, it was a mere concept; today it reaches hundreds of thousands and is having a profound impact on the villages, neighborhoods, islands, and schools where it is being vigorously implemented. This capacity for social transformation, increasingly being realized in the most advanced clusters, encompasses not just the work of community building but also the engagement of the believers, both in the discourses of society in all accessible social spaces as well as in projects of social and economic development.

The 25 February 2017 letter of your National Assembly written following consultations held at the Bahá'í World Centre is not intended simply to express a renewed concern with the challenges of race in your society and certainly not to introduce a new set of activities. It is a commitment to a path of systematic action and learning, involving community building, social action, and participation in the discourses of society, from which the community will never withdraw until the problems of race are completely resolved, no matter how long and difficult the path may be. Already your National Assembly is aware of the strivings of thousands of friends who, like yourself, are engaged in initiatives of varying scope and effectiveness along these lines; through systematization and learning there is every confidence that, as each year goes by, we will understand the issues involved more deeply, act more effectively, and enlarge the circle of those with whom we are engaged.

The House of Justice hopes that those friends in the United States who resolve to renew their commitment to uprooting racism and laying the basis for a society that reflects interracial harmony can draw insight and inspiration from the unwavering resolve of the Bahá'ís in Iran. The messages written to the friends there in recent years, most of which have been translated into English and are publicly available, are instructive in this regard. For almost two centuries, and particularly the last four decades of relentless oppression, the Bahá'ís in Iran have remained forward-looking, dynamic, vibrant, and committed to serving Iranian society. They have refused to allow apprehension and anxiety to take hold or let any calamity perturb their hearts. They have drawn on the highest reservoirs of solidarity and collaboration and responded to oppression with constructive resilience, eschewing despair, surrender, resentment, and hate and transcending mere survival, to transform conditions of ignorance and prejudice and win the respect and collaboration of their fair-minded countrymen. Those believers in the United States who have labored so persistently to promote race unity, especially the African American friends, should appreciate in their own efforts over the years the same expression of constructive resilience, born of their great love for Bahá'u'lláh, and see in the recent turmoil opportunity rather than obstacle. They cannot, as you know, respond to the current reality in the manner consuming most of their fellow citizens; they must, by word and by deed, elevate the existing conversation and set in motion constructive approaches that will prove ever more effective over time. Shoghi Effendi has explained that such problems as are now being witnessed are inevitable as the process of disintegration advances. "All humanity", a letter written on his behalf observes, "is disturbed and suffering and confused; we cannot expect to not be disturbed and not to suffer—but we don't have to be confused." The way forward has never been clearer, particularly with the new initiative of your National Assembly to organize these matters within the proven framework for action guiding the Bahá'í world's systematic endeavors.

From a letter to an individual, 4 February 2018

— *21* —

The House of Justice feels that the American believers' pursuit of the double crusade "to regenerate the inward life of their own community" and "to assail the long-standing evils that have entrenched themselves in the life of their nation" is something carried out as the friends execute their responsibilities for the Five Year Plan and is not something pursued apart from the Plan. In the same light, there is no program or special intervention that, if undertaken by the Bahá'í community, will free it from the challenge of racial prejudice as a first step before it can attempt to carry out successful efforts for the progress of the Faith. Rather, the capabilities of the believers to address the issues of racism afflicting themselves, their families, their communities, and the wider society will be cultivated hand in hand with other capabilities needed to advance the process of entry by troops as they learn to systematically pursue their efforts of community building, social action, and involvement in the discourses of society. In *The Advent of Divine Justice*, Shoghi Effendi states:

Freedom from racial prejudice, in any of its forms, should, at such a time as this when an increasingly large section of the human race is falling a victim to its devastating ferocity, be adopted as the watchword of the entire body of the American believers, in whichever state they reside, in whatever circles they move, whatever their age, traditions, tastes, and habits. It should be consistently demonstrated in every phase of their activity and life, whether in the Bahá'í community or outside it, in public or in private, formally as well as informally, individually as well as in their official capacity as organized groups, committees and Assemblies. It should be deliberately cultivated through the various and everyday opportunities, no matter how insignificant, that present themselves, whether in their homes, their business offices, their schools and colleges, their social parties and recreation grounds, their Bahá'í meetings, conferences, conventions, summer schools and Assemblies.

Here, the Guardian is calling for the friends to address the question of race unity as a part of life in all of the social spaces in which they are engaged, and, similarly, the House of Justice is now saying that freedom from racial prejudice must be the watchword of Bahá'ís in the social spaces in which they are engaged for the activities of the Plan. In such intimate settings, people of diverse racial backgrounds encounter the Word of God, and in their efforts to translate the Teachings into practical action, are able to generate bonds of love, affection, and unity, and to learn what it means to establish a true interracial fellowship that is powerful enough to overcome the forces of racism that afflict them and their society. Currently, among the Bahá'ís of the United States, race unity is a dimension of the work of community building in scores of clusters, of social action in hundreds of efforts of various levels of complexity, and of involvement in the discourses of society by thousands of believers in various settings. The House of Justice is confident that these endeavors will become more systematic, more widespread, and more effective as the learning process already set in motion by your National Spiritual Assembly is persistently pursued by the believers in greater numbers. Parallel with this, of course, is the effort of the National Assembly to engage at the national level in the discourse concerning race. In the same way as the other activities of the Plan, every challenge the community faces in the work of race unity will be overcome as capacity is raised among an expanding group of friends in each cluster through learning and systematic action.

Two additional points are offered for your consideration. As the Riḍván 2010 message of the House of Justice to the Bahá'ís of the world states:

... understanding the implications of the Revelation, both in terms of individual growth and social progress, increases manifold when study and service are joined and carried out concurrently. There, in the field of service, knowledge is tested, questions arise out of practice, and new levels of understanding are achieved.

The concept of the relationship of study and service clearly has relevance to the issues of promoting race unity and the growth of the Faith. The friends should study the Bahá'í writings on the subject of eliminating racial prejudice and familiarize themselves with the communications of the House of Justice on the current framework of action for growth. But study must be accompanied by action.

Moreover, obviously, the institutions of the Faith have an important role to play in promoting unity, and the House of Justice is pleased with the initiative your National Assembly has undertaken to assist the friends to understand how the framework for action of the Plan enables individuals, communities, and institutions to address, profoundly, the fragmentation in your nation that has been steadily intensifying in recent years, including on matters of race. However, it is, in the words of the beloved Guardian, "the individual believer on whom, in the last resort, depends the fate of the entire community." Therefore, the House of Justice encourages you to turn your attention away from what you believe are the inadequacies—real or perceived—of Bahá'í institutions in addressing the issues of concern to you and instead focus your spiritual and intellectual energies on the contribution that you, as an individual believer, can directly offer in service to the people in your immediate surroundings. It is hoped that you will advance in your own efforts with some like-minded friends in your local area to pursue your noble aims and to test and refine your ideas in practical action, raising up in turn others who will recognize Bahá'u'lláh and devote themselves to this vital work.

From a letter to an individual, 6 August 2018

— *22* —

The House of Justice highly appreciates the report of the actions you have taken since the gathering in the Holy Land in 2016 and the analysis of results and ongoing challenges. It feels that your assessment reinforces the importance of continuing to pursue the tasks summarized in the letter dated 30 December 2016 written on its behalf to which you refer in your letter. As you continue your noteworthy efforts to advance along the path laid out in that letter, you should keep in mind the fundamental difference between your work in the past to promote race unity and your efforts today. Whereas before you were implementing a centralized program initiated at the national level that involved friends across the country in what they easily understood to be a single endeavor, today, you are promoting a unity in diversity of actions, emerging largely from the grassroots, in pursuit of this aim. Many of the perceptions you describe can be understood in light of the difficulty in conveying how these seemingly unconnected elements all contribute to a common enterprise. Yet only through such a decentralized approach that is coherent with the framework for action of the Plan can the contribution of the American Bahá'í community to fundamental, sustained, spiritual and social transformation gradually grow in scale and effectiveness—through action and reflection over time—until it has a profound effect on the wider society.

As your own analysis shows, there are advantages to sometimes working in multiracial spaces and at other times to spaces for African Americans alone. In pursuing a two-pronged approach to community building within a cluster, some gatherings will take place in neighborhoods and some in a locality or at the cluster level. These can be organized in different ways to meet different needs. Even with neighborhoods, some will involve an interracial population and others will not. But you should not underestimate the value of contributing to spiritual empowerment and community building in an African American neighborhood where the work of a few dedicated friends can lead to the participation of scores of families—an experience that can itself radically alter and revive a local Bahá'í community that showed no previous capacity to deal with matters of race.

With these points in mind, you are free to determine, after thorough consultation with the Counsellors, the most effective way to arrange gatherings of African American friends to achieve your purpose. Should you ultimately decide to create a national conference, it should not be simply as an end in itself but should serve as a means for accelerating the work of community building, social action, and involvement in the discourses of society. For as the

House of Justice has emphasized in previous communications, it is not predominantly by means of offering special courses and programs on race within the Bahá'í community that racial issues will be overcome. Instead, it is through collective action in the various social spaces in which the friends are wholeheartedly engaged to translate the Teachings into action that they will, through mistakes and difficulties, with love and forbearance, learn to resolve challenges pertaining to race, both within their communities and in the society at large.

Finally, the highly meritorious work of your Office of Public Affairs in furthering your national discourse is noted with appreciation. No doubt, a significant body of experience and understanding has now been accumulated about the nature of the current discourse on race in the United States, the receptivity to specific Bahá'í concepts, the nature of certain pitfalls to avoid, and insights into the type of language that must be utilized to surmount the increasing polarization on this issue even among fair-minded and sympathetic citizens. When you feel the time is right, you can draw upon this experience and understanding not only to implement the anticipated national gathering for leaders of thought but also to prepare any public statement on the subject of race unity and the future of the American nation.

From a letter to the National Spiritual Assembly
of the United States, 24 March 2019

— 23 —

The House of Justice sympathizes with your deep concern about the issues you have raised and acknowledges your sincerity and desire to see the Bahá'í community and the wider society make progress with addressing these challenges. It encourages you not to become disheartened by any problems you encounter. As Shoghi Effendi explained, "the promised glories" envisioned by Bahá'u'lláh "can be revealed only in the fullness of time"; it is our test and privilege at this juncture in the Formative Age to learn how to systematically propagate His teachings and translate them into effective action as a remedy for the world's multiplying ills.

The House of Justice is confident that you can trust that your

110

fellow believers, who faithfully embrace Bahá'u'lláh's principle of the oneness of humanity, share your longing for the complete elimination of racial prejudice. Yet, Bahá'ís are not immune from the negative forces operating in society at large, which may result in misunderstandings and a delay in responding to challenges. At this time, the people of the United States do not have unity of thought and vision about how the problem of racial prejudice can be resolved; they are, instead, divided socially and politically on this issue. As you witness, even among Black intellectuals, as well as within the African American community more generally, there are disparate views. Therefore, rather than becoming enmeshed in patterns of behavior pervasive in the wider society that seek to assign blame or deal with issues at the level of broad generalities, Bahá'ís have the opportunity to address the challenge of racial prejudice through the instrumentality of the teachings of Bahá'u'lláh and His Administrative Order. They do so by concentrating on practical challenges in specific settings through consultation in an atmosphere of love and common purpose.

Every believer can address the improvement of his or her own character. Each can strive to work alongside others to ensure that the social spaces in which they participate—especially in families, local communities, places of work and education, Bahá'í activities, Spiritual Assemblies, and committees—manifest freedom from prejudice in all its forms. Furthermore, the framework for action of the current Plan enables the believers to expand the reach of these efforts by engaging others in neighborhoods and clusters in the process of community building, initiatives for social action, and the prevalent discourses of society. In these contexts, when a specific concern is identified, the believers and their friends can explore the problem together and then participate in a process of learning how to resolve it, while eschewing any inclination toward withdrawal or conflict. Thus, day by day, in practical ways, they learn to solve particular problems that arise and at the same time build capacity to address more complex issues.

As the friends around the world have adopted this approach to address problems in diverse societies, promising signs are already appearing in many places where the Plan's framework for action has taken root. For example, in the Bihar Sharif cluster in India, the oppressive influence of the centuries-old caste system is gradually being undone at the grassroots. The communities in this cluster are learning to mix without regard to caste, so much so that the friends are visiting the homes of families from different castes. To cite another example, in the Lubumbashi cluster in the Democratic Republic of the Congo, the inequality between the sexes has long prevented women from speaking in the presence of men in various social spaces. Now, however, women have been given the courage to freely share their ideas and consult with men in different settings.

You indicate that you have decided to focus on spreading the Faith among African Americans and to dedicate yourself to their advancement and upliftment. This will, no doubt, allow you to learn how to create a social space for individuals to come together in a new pattern of engagement. The House of Justice hopes that you might find one or two other like-minded believers who can assist you in applying the instruments and methods of the Plan to cultivate a dynamic and growing pattern of community life. In this regard, when reaching out to those from the wider community, you can present the message of Bahá'u'lláh as the healing remedy for the ills of humanity and invite the receptive souls you encounter to become protagonists of a constant effort to learn to apply His teachings effectively, explaining that Bahá'ís are also learning to walk this same path. As 'Abdu'l-Bahá is reported to have remarked: "The earth plane is a workshop, not an art gallery for the exhibits of perfect powers. This is not the plane of perfection, but earth is the crucible for refining and moulding character".

From a letter to an individual, 15 December 2020

— *24* —

Sadly, at the current time, instead of a united effort to resolve the remaining challenges pertaining to racial prejudice in America, the matter all too often takes the form of political or contentious debate—whose aim is contest and the effort to defeat opposing views. In this perspective, thoughtful ideas that may provide insights useful to effecting lasting social change are distorted and exaggerated to emphasize divisions and make constructive exchange of views impossible. This has occurred with certain concepts and with ideas of particular thinkers, making it difficult to evaluate any merit they may contain without being drawn into a polarizing debate. Bahá'u'lláh has counselled His followers "not to view with too critical an eye the sayings and writings of men. Let them rather approach such sayings and writings in a spirit of open-mindedness and loving sympathy." Therefore, the friends are advised to avoid two extremes: either uncritically accepting every theory put forward, or dismissing entirely every theory because it falls short of the Bahá'í teachings or has flaws within it. Rather, it would be more helpful for the believers to consider such ideas as contributions to a public consultation that seeks to identify solutions to the problem of racial prejudice. Insights could then be drawn by the friends which they find to be compatible with the teachings to enhance their own efforts.

While the methods and approaches adopted by believers may vary—some seeing value in certain ideas from the wider society with which others may disagree—the friends should not allow differing opinions to become a point of dispute and contention in the community. And of course, there is no justification for the vilification of any group of people. What is clear, and has been emphasized by both 'Abdu'l-Bahá and Shoghi Effendi, is the imperative that the races work together to eradicate racial prejudice. As mentioned in our letter to you dated 27 October 2020, the House of Justice has advised the friends in your country that, in the process of learning how to respond to the challenge of racial prejudice, it is not possible for them to "effect the transformation envisioned by Bahá'u'lláh merely by adopting the perspectives, practices, concepts, criticisms, and language of contemporary society." Instead, their approach "will be distinguished by maintaining a humble posture of learning, weighing alternatives in the light of His teachings, consulting to harmonize differing views and shape collective action, and marching forward with unbreakable unity in serried lines."

As the friends work together to remove the blight of racism from society, challenges will no doubt arise; however, through patience as well as love for one another, it will be possible for them to encourage and support each other to reflect deeply on their own obligation to deal with the issue of racial prejudice. In such a culture, each individual can personally assess, in an atmosphere of uncensorious forbearance, his or her own condition and possibilities for improvement. In this way, all can grow together and develop their capacities in an environment characterized by tender affection, reciprocity, and cooperation, in which the friends do not sit in judgment of their fellow believers but, rather, urge each other to contribute their share to the establishment of the World Order of Bahá'u'lláh.

It is also important to remember that this is the Formative Age of the Faith and, as Shoghi Effendi stated, "the promised glories" envisioned by Bahá'u'lláh "can be revealed only in the fullness of time"; it is our test and privilege at this juncture to learn how to systematically propagate His teachings and translate them into effective action as a remedy for the world's multiplying ills. You are therefore encouraged not to become disheartened or discouraged by any problems you may encounter but, rather, see them as opportunities for learning and progress. This can be challenging, especially if we feel that our fellow believers are not living up to the teachings in the way we understand them. However, we should bear in mind that, despite any general difficulties, each believer has the obligation to strive to do what is right. Thus, as Shoghi Effendi explained:

You must not make the great mistake of judging our Faith by one community which obviously needs to study and obey the Bahá'í teachings. Human frailties and peculiarities can be a great test. But the only way, or perhaps I should say the first and best way, to remedy such situations, is to oneself do what is right. One soul can be the cause of the spiritual illumination of a continent. Now that you have seen, and remedied, a great fault in your own life, now that you see more clearly what is lacking in your own community, there is nothing to prevent you from arising and showing such an example, such a love and spirit of service, as to enkindle the hearts of your fellow Bahá'ís.

He urges you to study deeply the teachings, teach others, study with those Bahá'ís who are anxious to do so, the deeper teachings of our Faith, and through example, effort and prayer, bring about a change.

From a letter to an individual, 29 July 2021

Works Cited

'Abdu'l-Bahá. *Bahá'í World Faith*, US Bahá'í Publishing Trust, 1956.

———. *The Promulgation of Universal Peace: Talks Delivered by 'Abdu'l-Bahá during His Visit to the United States and Canada in 1912*. Compiled by Howard MacNutt, 2nd ed., US Bahá'í Publishing Trust, 1982.

———. *Selections from the Writings of 'Abdu'l-Bahá*. US Bahá'í Publishing Trust, 1978.

———. *Tablets of the Divine Plan*. US Bahá'í Publishing Trust, 1993.

Baker, Lee D. Savage to Negro: Anthropology and the Construction of Race, 1896-1954, University of California Press, Berkeley and Los Angeles, 1998. https://a.co/0dByFp1

Bahá'u'lláh. *Epistle to the Son of the Wolf*. Translated by Shoghi Effendi, US Bahá'í Publishing Trust, 1988.

———. *Tablets of Bahá'u'lláh*. US Bahá'í Publishing Trust, 1994.

———. *Tabernacle of Unity*. Haifa: Bahá'í World Centre, 2006.

Bookman, Jay. "Let's Be Honest about who Really Fans the Flame of Racism," *Georgia Recorder*, 30 May 2020. georgiarecorder.com/2020/05/30/bookman-claim-that-obama-made-people-racist-fuels-flames-of-discord/

Freeman, Morgan. "Morgan Freeman on Black History Month." *YouTube*, uploaded by rickey2b4, 29 Apr. 2009, www.youtube.com/watch?v=GeixtYS-P3s&t

Friedersdorf, Conor. "Why California Rejected Racial Preferences, Again," *The Atlantic*, November 10, 2020.

Hatcher, William S. *Love, Power, and Justice: The Dynamics of Authentic Morality*, Wilmette: Bahá'í Publishing Trust, 1998.

Hughes, Coleman. "A Better Anti-Racism", *Manhattan Institute*, 19 August 2020. www.manhattan-institute.org/a-better-anti-racism.

———. *The End of Race Politics: Arguments for a Colorblind America*. Penguin Random House, 2024.

Kendi, Ibram X. *How to be an Antiracist*. New York: One World, 2019.

Kendi, Ibram X. *Stamped from the Beginning: The Definitive History of Racist Ideas in America*, Bold Type Books, New York, 2016.

Marks, Rachel, Nicholas Jones, and Karen Battle. "What Updates to OMB's Race/Ethnicity Standards Mean for the Census Bureau." *United States Census Bureau*, 8 Apr. 2024, www.census.gov/newsroom/blogs/random-samplings/2024/04/updates-race-ethnicity-standards.html

Mason, Sheena Michele. *The Raceless Antiracist: Why Ending Race Is the Future of Antiracism*, Pitchstone Publishing, 2024.

National Spiritual Assembly of the Bahá'ís of the United States, *A Spiritual Path to Unity and Social Justice: The Bahá'í Faith in America*, 2021. sites.google.com/bahai.us/race-unity-action

Office of Public Information, United States. Unpublished paper.

Roberts, Dorothy. *Fatal Invention: How Science, Politics, and Big Business Recreate Race in the Twenty-first Century*. The New Press, 2012.

Ross, Michael E. "Black History Month: Has It Run Its Course?" *NBC News*, 1 Feb. 2006, www.nbcnews.com/id/wbna10990868

Shoghi Effendi. *The Advent of Divine Justice*. US Bahá'í Publishing Trust, 1984.

———. *Bahá'í Administration: Selected Messages 1922–1932*. US Bahá'í Publishing Trust, 1998.

———. *Citadel of Faith*. US Bahá'í Publishing Trust, 1980.

———. *Compilation of Compilations*. Vol. 2., Bahá'í Publications Australia, 1991.

———. *The World Order of Bahá'u'lláh*. US Bahá'í Publishing Trust, 1974.

The Universal House of Justice. *Framework for Action: Selected Messages of the Universal House of Justice and Supplementary Material, 2006–2016*. Palabra Publications, 2017.

———. *Messages of the Universal House of Justice: 1963-1986*. US Bahá'í Publishing Trust, 1996.

———. *Messages of the Universal House of Justice: 2001-2022*. US Bahá'í Publishing Trust, 2024.

———. *Reflections on the First Century of the Formative Age*. Bahá'í World Centre, 2023.

The Universal House of Justice. *Turning Point: Selected Messages of the Universal House of Justice and Supplementary Material, 1996–2006.* Palabra Publications, 2006.

———. To the Bahá'ís of the Democratic Republic of the Congo, 1 November 2022.

———. Letter written on behalf of Universal House of Justice, 4 February 2018.

———. Letter written on behalf of Universal House of Justice, 6 August 2018.

———. Letter written on behalf of Universal House of Justice, 24 March 2019.

———. Letter written on behalf of Universal House of Justice, 15 December 2020.

———. Letter written on behalf of Universal House of Justice, 19 December 2020.

Further Reading

Allen, Theodore W. *The Invention of the White Race.* Verso, 2012.

Alexander, Michelle. *The New Jim Crow: Mass Incarceration in the Age of Colorblindness.* The New Press, 2010.

Appiah, Kwame Anthony. *The Lies That Blind: Rethinking Identity: Creed, Country, Color, Class, Culture.* Liveright Publishing Company, 2018.

Baldwin, James. "On Being White . . . And Other Lies," *Essence*, April 1984.

Bonilla-Silva, Eduardo. *Racism without Racists: Color-Blind Racism and the Persistence of Racial Inequality in America.* Rowman and Littlefield, 2022.

DiAngelo, Robin. *White Fragility: Why It's So Hard for White People to Talk About Racism.* Beacon Press, 2018.

Lample, Paul. "Toward a Framework for Action," *Journal of Bahá'í Studies*, vol. 28, no. 3, 2018, pp. 11–53. doi: 10.31581/jbs-28.3.2(2018).

Mahiri, Jabari. *Deconstructing Race: Multicultural Education Beyond the Color-Bind.* Teachers College Press, 2017.

Masuoka, Natalie. *Multiracial Identity and Racial Politics in the United States*. Oxford UP, 2017.

McCarthy, Thomas. *Race, Empire, and the Idea of Human Development*. Cambridge UP, 2009.

McWhorter, John. *Woke Racism: How a New Religion Has Betrayed Black America*. Penguin Random House, 2021.

Mills, Charles W. *The Racial Contract*. Cornell UP, 1997.

Prewitt, Kenneth. "Racial Classification in America: Where Do We Go from Here?" *Daedalus*, vol. 134, no. 1, 2005, pp. 5–17.

Putnam, Robert. With Shaylyn Romney Garrett. *The Upswing: How America Came Together a Century Ago and How We Can Do It Again*. Simon and Schuster, 2021.

Rose, Tricia. *Metaracism: How Systemic Racism Devastates Black Lives—And How We Break Free*. Basic Books, 2024.

Salam, Reihan. "America Needs Anti-racialism", *The Atlantic*, 26 May 2022.   www.theatlantic.com/ideas/archive/2022/05/anti-racialism-ibram-kendi-anti-racism/638433/.

Snipp, Matthew C. "Racial Measurement in the American Census: Past Practices and Implications for the Future," *Annual Review of Psychology*, vol. 29, 2003, pp. 563–588.   www.jstor.org/stable/30036980

Solórzano, Daniel G. and Lindsay Peréz Huber. *Racial Microaggressions: Using Critical Race Theory to Respond to Everyday Racism*. Teacher's College Press, 2020.

Thompson, Chalmer E. and Robert T. Carter, ed. *Racial Identity Theory: Applications to Individual, Group, and Organizational Interventions*. Routledge, 2012.

Waithaka, Wairimu Maureen and Muriithi Benjamin. "Learning to be Black: Navigating a New Identity in Nova Scotia," *CBC News*, 11 February 2021.   www.cbc.ca/news/canada/nova-scotia/learning-to-be-black-1.5909024.

Wilkerson, Isabel. *Caste: The Origins of Our Discontents*. Random House, 2023.

Yacovone, David. *Teaching White Supremacy: America's Democratic Ordeal and the Forging of Our National Identity*. Pantheon Books, 2022.

Zack, Naomi. *Philosophy of Race: An Introduction*. Palgrave, 2018.

www.ingramcontent.com/pod-product-compliance
Lightning Source LLC
Chambersburg PA
CBHW072145020426
42334CB00018B/1892